Birds of
ARUBA, CURAÇAO, AND BONAIRE

Birds of
ARUBA, CURAÇAO, AND BONAIRE

Bart de Boer, Eric Newton,
and Robin Restall

PRINCETON UNIVERSITY PRESS
PRINCETON AND OXFORD

Princeton Field Guides

Rooted in field experience and scientific study, Princeton's guides to animals and plants are the authority for professional scientists and amateur naturalists alike. **Princeton Field Guides** present this information in a compact format carefully designed for easy use in the field. The guides illustrate every species in color and provide detailed information on identification, distribution, and biology.

Related Titles:

Birds of East Africa: Kenya, Tanzania, Uganda, Rwanda, and Burundi, by Terry Stevenson and John Fanshawe
Birds of Kenya and Northern Tanzania: Field Guide Edition, by Dale A. Zimmerman, Donald A. Turner, and David J. Pearson
Birds of Southern Africa, by Ian Sinclair, Phil Hockey, and Warwick Tarboton
Birds of Western Africa, by Nik Borrow and Ron Demey
Birds of the Horn of Africa, by Nigel Redman, Terry Stevenson, and John Fanshawe
Birds of the Middle East, by Richard Porter and Simon Aspinall
Birds of Australia, by Ken Simpson and Nicolas Day
Birds of Borneo: Brunei, Sabah, Sarawak, and Kalimantan, by Susan Myers
Birds of Europe, by Lars Svensson, Dan Zetterström, and Killian Mullarney
Birds of Melanesia: Bismarcks, Solomons, Vanuatu, and New Caledonia, by Guy Dutson
Birds of Peru, by Thomas S. Schulenberg, Douglas F. Stotz, Daniel F. Lane, John P. O'Neill, and Theodore A. Parker III

Published in the United States, Canada, and the Philippine Islands in 2012 by
Princeton University Press, 41 William Street, Princeton, New Jersey 08540

nathist.press.princeton.edu

Published in the United Kingdom and European Union in 2011 by
Christopher Helm, an imprint of Bloomsbury Publishing plc, 50 Bedford Square, London, WC1B 3DP

Copyright © 2011 text by Bart de Boer and Eric Newton
Copyright © 2011 illustrations by Robin Restall

The right of Bart de Boer, Eric Newton, and Robin Restall to be identified as the authors of this work has been asserted by them in accordance with the Copyright, Design and Patents Act 1988.

Library of Congress Control Number 2011935843
ISBN 978-0-691-15336-0

All rights reserved. No part of this publication may be reproduced or used in any form or by any means – photographic, electronic or mechanical, including photocopying, recording, taping or information storage or retrieval systems – without permission of the publishers.

Design by Julie Dando at Fluke Art

Printed and bound in China by C&C Offset Printing Co Ltd

10 9 8 7 6 5 4 3 2 1

Cover artwork
Front and back: Ruby-topaz Hummingbird

CONTENTS

	Plate	Page
INTRODUCTION		9
GENERAL FLORA AND FAUNA		11
THE AVIFAUNA		12
HOW TO USE THIS BOOK		14
BIRD TOPOGRAPHY		15
THE ISLANDS AND THEIR SPECIAL BIRDING SITES		17
Aruba		17
Curaçao		18
Bonaire		19
CONSERVATION		20
LOCAL NAMES		20
PLATES AND SPECIES ACCOUNTS		22
Quails ODONTOPHORIDAE	1	22
Ducks and Geese ANATIDAE	1–5	22–30
Cormorants PHALACROCORACIDAE	6	32
Pelicans PELECANIDAE	6	32
Petrels and Shearwaters PROCELLARIIDAE	7	34
Storm-petrels HYDROBATIDAE	7	34
Tropicbirds PHAETHONTIDAE	8	36
Flamingos PHOENICOPTERIDAE	8	36
Frigatebirds FREGATIDAE	9	38
Boobies SULIDAE	10	40
Herons, Bitterns and Egrets ARDEIDAE	11–14	42–48
Grebes PODICIPEDIDAE	14	48
Ibises and Spoonbills THRESKIORNITHIDAE	15–16	50–52
Storks CICONIIDAE	16	52
New World Vultures CATHARTIDAE	16	52
Osprey PANDIONIDAE	16	52
Hawks and Kites ACCIPITRIDAE	17	54
Caracaras and Falcons FALCONIDAE	18	56
Rails and Gallinules RALLIDAE	19	58
Limpkin ARAMIDAE	20	60

Thick-knees BURHINIDAE	20	60
Lapwings and Plovers CHARADRIIDAE	20–21	60–62
Sungrebe HELIORNITHIDAE	22	64
Jacanas JACANIDAE	22	64
Stilts and Avocets RECURVIROSTRIDAE	22	64
Oystercatchers HAEMATOPODIDAE	22	64
Sandpipers and Allies SCOLOPACIDAE	23–27	66–74
Skuas and Jaegers STERCORARIIDAE	27–28	74–76
Gulls LARINAE	29–31	78–82
Terns STERNINAE	32–35	84–90
Skimmers RYNCHOPIDAE	36	92
Pigeons and Doves COLUMBIDAE	37–38	94–96
Parrots, Parakeets and Macaws PSITTACIDAE	39–40	98–100
Cuckoos CUCULIDAE	41	102
Barn Owls TYTONIDAE	42	104
Owls STRIGIDAE	42	104
Oilbird STEATORNITHIDAE	42	104
Nightjars and Nighthawks CAPRIMULGIDAE	43–44	106–108
Swifts APODIDAE	44	108
Hummingbirds TROCHILIDAE	45	110
Kingfishers ALCEDINIDAE	46	112
Woodpeckers PICIDAE	47	114
Tyrant Flycatchers TYRANNIDAE	47–50	114–120
Vireos VIREONIDAE	51	122
Swallows and Martins HIRUNDINIDAE	52–54	124–128
Chats and Old World Flycatchers MUSCICAPIDAE	55	130
Thrushes TURDIDAE	55	130
Waxwings BOMBYCILLIDAE	56	132
Mockingbirds and Thrashers MIMIDAE	56	132
New World Warblers PARULIDAE	57–63	134–146
Bananaquit and Grassquits INCERTAE SEDIS	63, 67	146, 154
Tanagers THRAUPIDAE	64–65	148–150
Weavers PLOCEIDAE	65	150
Old World Sparrows PASSERIDAE	65	150
Cardinal Grosbeaks and Allies CARDINALIDAE	66	152

Seedeaters and Allies EMBERIZIDAE	67	154
Starlings STURNIDAE	68	156
New World Blackbirds ICTERIDAE	68–70	156–160

APPENDIX:
   Introduced parrots and parakeets   162
   Occasional escapees   162
CHECKLIST OF THE BIRDS OF ARUBA, CURAÇAO AND BONAIRE   163
BIBLIOGRAPHY   171
INDEX   173

INTRODUCTION

The islands of Aruba, Curaçao and Bonaire lie off the north coast of South America in the southern part of the Caribbean Sea. The geological basis of these islands was formed by volcanic oozing on the bottom of the ocean in the Cretaceous era (about 80 million years ago). The collision of the South American tectonic plate against the Caribbean plate caused uplifting of these sea-bottom volcanic formations and formed the islands. As the rock reached the sea surface coral reefs started to grow during the Pleistocene era (more than one million years ago). The reefs were subsequently lifted up, and because of the oscillating sea level during the different ice ages, limestone terraces were formed. These still remain along the coasts of the islands, particularly the northern coast.

Aruba has a surface area of approximately 190km^2 and lies about 30km north of the Venezuelan peninsula of Paraguaná. Curaçao is 75km to the east of Aruba and 66km north of the Venezuelan coast – it has a surface area of approximately 444km^2 including the satellite island of Klein Curaçao 11km to the east. Bonaire is 55km to the east of Curaçao and 88km north of the Venezuelan coast, and has a surface area of approximately 288km^2 including Klein Bonaire.

The climate of the islands is semi-arid, with distinct dry and rainy seasons. The dry season runs from February to June and the rainy season from September to January. Aruba is the driest island with a mean annual rainfall of 410mm; Curaçao has a mean annual rainfall of 555mm and Bonaire 465mm. These are means over several years, but the annual rainfall can vary greatly from year to year. The higher areas of the islands have a slightly higher precipitation than the lower, which is reflected in the vegetation of particularly the western part of Curaçao and the northern areas of Bonaire. The average temperature is about 28°C, with about 24°C at night in January to 33°C midday in September, the hottest month (when an exceptional temperature of 38°C has been measured). On very cold days the temperature can drop down to around 20°C. The wind is mostly quite constant and brisk from the east to north-east – the north-eastern trade wind. The wind direction changes only occasionally.

The first known human inhabitants of the islands arrived almost 5,000 years ago; these were small groups which had no agriculture and subsisted on whatever they could get from the wild. Around 1,500 years ago

came the Caquetios, a tribe which did have agriculture, enabling them to live a more settled life in larger groups. The Caquetios were still on the islands when the Spanish arrived in 1499 and took possession of the islands. The Caquetio language from the Arawak group still lingers today in some words, including some local bird names. As no gold was found and the area was arid, the Spanish had little interest in the islands and only had a limited presence.

In 1634 the islands were seized from Spain by the Dutch West India Company, which was looking for a stopover on the return route to Europe from their colonies in northern Brazil, but they were also interested in the available salt, as salt was important to cure their own commodity, herring. Soon they were also using the islands, particularly Curaçao, as a depot for their transatlantic slave trade. Although very early on in the 17th century the Dutch were against the slave trade, greed was to trump principle.

By the last half of the 18th century the slave trade slowed down. Now the island of Curaçao, and especially its sister island of St Eustatius in the north-eastern Caribbean, were used as free ports. In those times a free port did not mean duty-free shopping for tourists, but a place where any ship of any flag would come to trade with anybody, subverting the colonial rulings that they could only trade colonial commodities with their respective motherland.

By the end of the 18th century the Dutch West India Company was disbanded and the islands came under direct rule of the Netherlands. This remained the situation (with the exception of a few years of British rule during Napoleonic times) until 1954. In that year the Statute of the Kingdom of the Netherlands came into force. This charter created a new Kingdom comprising three countries: the Netherlands; Suriname; and the Netherlands Antilles, formed by Aruba, Curaçao, Bonaire and three islands in the north-eastern Caribbean: St Maarten, St Eustatius and Saba.

According to the Statute, each country has its own government to take care of everything except defence and foreign affairs, which are Kingdom tasks. The Kingdom government consists of the ministers from the government of the Netherlands, to which a minister plenipotentiary is added from each of the other countries. The Kingdom government is supervised by the parliament of the Netherlands, although members of the parliament of the other countries are occasionally involved in decision-making. The Kingdom is not only responsible for defence and foreign affairs, but also guarantees good governance and human rights in the whole Kingdom.

In 1975 Suriname stepped out of the Kingdom and became an independent republic. In 1986 Aruba left the Netherlands Antilles, instead taking the place of Suriname as a country within the Kingdom. Then in 2010 the Netherlands Antilles were dissolved and both Curaçao and St Maarten became countries within the Kingdom alongside Aruba and the Netherlands, while Bonaire, St Eustatius and Saba became part of the Netherlands as special municipalities. However, the same Court of Justice still functions for all six Caribbean islands of the Kingdom.

Aruba and Curaçao (with St Maarten) each has its own currency, the Aruban florin and the Caribbean guilder, while Bonaire and the other two islands now use the US dollar as their official currency. As the Netherlands uses the Euro, there are four official currencies in the Kingdom.

GENERAL FLORA AND FAUNA

The vegetation of the islands is largely dictated by the semi-dry climate. Very obvious are the large candelabra cacti; all three species (*Cereus repandus*, *Stenocereus griseus* and the less common *Pilosocereus lanuginosus*) are restricted to these islands and northern Venezuela, as is the very common Prickly Pear (*Opuntia wentiana*). Other dominant deciduous and spiny trees include *Prosopis juliflora* and *Acacia tortuosa*, which have a wider distribution. A typical tree is *Caesalpinia coriaria*, which grows asymmetrically according to the predominant wind direction. On the islands the name used most often for this tree is 'Watapana', while the pods from which tannin is extracted are called 'Dividivi'. Both names are from Arawak, but the latter name is more widely used nowadays for the tree in a more popular context.

On the flat coastal limestone plains on the north-eastern coasts, exposed to strong winds and oceanic spray, the vegetation is low, including plant species which grow taller inland.

One habitat which supports a diverse bird population is that formed by the mangroves fringing inland lagoons. Red mangroves with prop roots grow in the shallow protected water, while black mangroves with pneumatophores, small upright root branches rising clear of the water, are found in the more muddy areas.

Red mangroves with prop roots.

Black mangroves with pneumatophores.

Land snail Cerion sp.; each island has its own species.

The terrestrial fauna is typified by snails and lizards. The air-breathing snail genus *Cerion* is endemic to the Caribbean region (though absent from Jamaica, Central and South America and the eastern Lesser Antilles). Each island has its own species or subspecies and often several, depending on its geological history. For Curaçao six (sub)species are recognised, for Bonaire two and Aruba one.

Each island has its own species or subspecies of the ubiquitous whiptail lizards or, in the case of Aruba several, although some of those are shared with the mainland. Aruba and Curaçao share an endemic anole lizard, while Bonaire has a species of its own. The Green Iguana has a much wider distribution. All the islands have various species of geckos, several of which are endemic whilst others have a wider distribution. One species (House Gecko) has been introduced.

The only native snake on Bonaire is a small blind one. Curaçao has a different species of blind snake and an endemic species of typical snake. Aruba has another native typical snake, but also an endemic subspecies of rattlesnake. However, the boa constrictor has recently been introduced on Aruba where it has multiplied dramatically and appears to have a great negative influence on the bird life. Sometimes they can be seen just under the top of a candelabra cactus, waiting for a bird to perch on the top.

Only Aruba, which was at one time (almost) connected to the mainland, has a native amphibian, a small toad. These have been introduced to the other two islands during the 20th century. Recently whistling frogs have been introduced through the importation of plants.

The only native mammals on all three islands are several species of bats. Additionally Aruba and Curaçao have a small vesper mouse and a species of cottontail rabbit. On Curaçao you may still see the White-tailed Deer. Introduced mammals comprise rats, House Mice and cats, but thankfully no mongooses.

THE AVIFAUNA

In general, the native bird fauna of the islands is considered to be South American, as would be expected considering the proximity of the mainland. However, there is also a strong West Indian element, most marked in Bonaire and least in Aruba. This attribute of the islands' birdlife was recognised in the 19th century. Hartert (1893) noted the stronger affinity of the bird species of Bonaire, and to a lesser extent Curaçao, to those of the northern islands of the Caribbean, particularly the Virgin Islands.

The species Hartert mentioned as being more 'West Indian' were the Pearly-eyed Thrasher (*Margarops fuscatus*), Grasshopper Sparrow (*Ammodramus savannorum*), Caribbean Elaenia (*Elaenia martinica*) and Grey Kingbird (*Tyrannus dominicensis*). Furthermore, he noted that the Bananaquit (*Coereba flaveola*) subspecies of

Aruba, Curaçao and Bonaire had more similarities with those from the Virgin Islands than with those from the closer Lesser Antilles. Strangely, he also included in this analysis the Troupial (*Icterus icterus*) and Brown-throated Parakeet (*Aratinga pertinax*), species which are definitely South American and probably introduced in the Virgin Islands from Curaçao. The Troupial did not occur on Bonaire until it was introduced from Curaçao in the early 1970s.

Besides resident birds and seabirds that breed on the islands or nearby, there are visitors and vagrants from the south and migrants from the north: several species of shorebirds, waterfowl, and many warblers. This guide describes all the warblers that have so far been recorded on the islands, but sooner or later probably all North American migrant warblers will be recorded. Aruba, Curaçao and Bonaire lie due south from the large expanse of the Caribbean Sea. The major migratory routes are on either side, through Central America or through the Eastern Caribbean island chain. This means that the islands do not receive very large numbers of migrating birds, but off-course visitors from both flyways can arrive, providing unexpected records.

If you think you have seen a bird that is not mentioned in this guide for that island, you can report this to birds@carmabi.org, preferably with a photograph. For general recording of your bird sightings and to share your data, a good resource is eBird: http://ebird.org/content/caribbean.

Coastal habitat after heavy rain.

Same area at the end of the dry season.

HOW TO USE THIS BOOK

The taxonomy and nomenclature used in this book mainly follows those of the American Ornithologists Union (AOU) and its South American Checklist Committee (SACC). The sequence of birds in the species accounts sometimes differs from the SACC list in order to achieve a logical plate design. A full checklist of the birds of the islands, in SACC sequence, is given on pages 163–170.

MEASUREMENTS
The length (**L**) of each species is given in centimetres. The wingspan (**W**) is also given for a few groups, such as seabirds, herons and some raptors.

SPECIES ACCOUNTS
Each species account begins with the common name in English followed by the scientific name. The local names (where relevant) are given according to the orthography of each island. The names of subspecies (ssp.), if determined, are mentioned in the text.

The species accounts give a concise description of each species, with key identification features highlighted in bold italics. Information is also provided on vocalisations (**Voice**), habitat and habits (**HH**), and status and abundance (**Status**). Some alternative names [Alt] are given at the end, and a taxonomic note (**Note**) if relevant.

Voice: in addition to the description of the vocalisation of each species, the website www.xeno-canto.org provides sound files for many species. It should be taken into account that there is regional variation in the vocalisation of many species.

Status: the general status of a species refers to its occurrence on the islands and whether it breeds.

Resident birds are recorded frequently throughout the year and most will breed on the islands; some non-breeding birds present throughout the year will breed in the region.

Regular visitors are migrants which are seen every year, mainly during the northern (boreal) winter. Migrants from South America are seen during the southern (austral) winter.

Irregular visitors are not seen every year but occasionally may turn up in considerable numbers, depending on weather conditions.

Rare visitors are only seen exceptionally, although their true status may be clouded by lack of observer coverage.

Abundance: due to the small size of the islands and the relative uniformity of the habitat, most birds may be seen throughout the islands. Only when a species is restricted to a special habitat is it mentioned as such. For most birds, only general descriptions of their habitats have been given (e.g. freshwater ponds for waterbirds) and their abundance is clearly linked to these habitats.

THE PLATES
The plates have been designed especially for this book. Many of the images have been taken from *Birds of Northern South America* (Restall *et al.* 2006) or *Birds of Trinidad & Tobago* 2nd edition (Kenefick *et al.* 2011). Some new images have been painted specifically for this book. All artwork is by Robin Restall.

BIRD TOPOGRAPHY

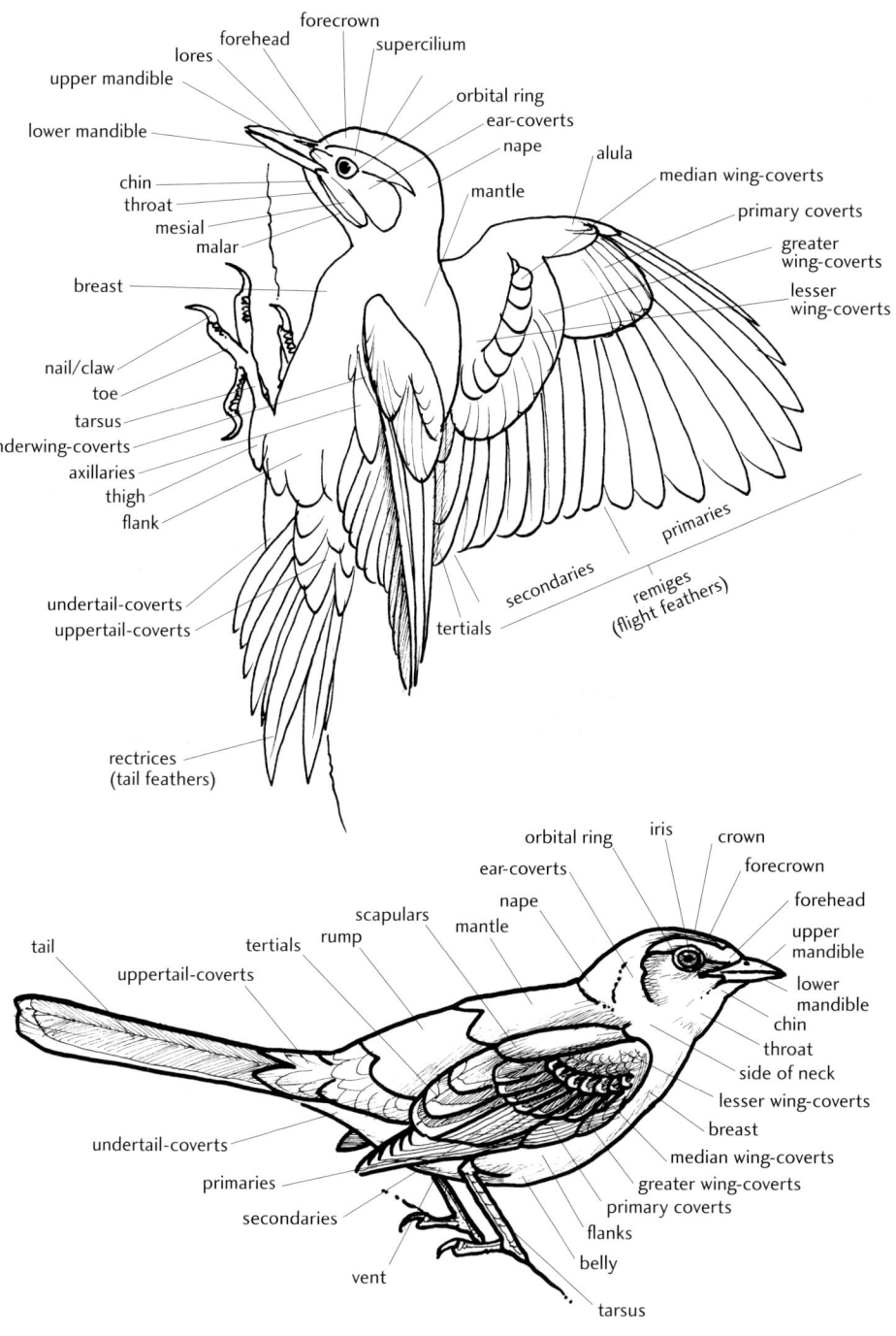

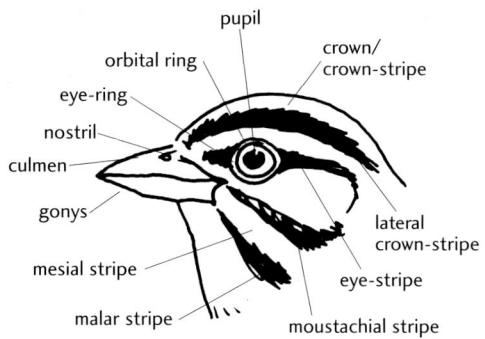

THE ISLANDS AND THEIR SPECIAL BIRDING SITES

On each of the islands there are many special areas to watch birds. Of course, you will see birds everywhere, from the introduced Rock Pigeon and House Sparrow which are taking over the inner cities, to the Bananaquits and Bare-eyed Pigeons in the residential areas, including around hotels.

BirdLife International has published a list of Important Bird Areas (IBA) for the Caribbean (BirdLife International, 2008). These IBAs, however, are primarily a management and conservation tool; often they are breeding areas for vulnerable birds. To avoid disturbance, it would not be appropriate to enter these breeding areas during breeding time, especially at sites where terns and flamingos nest.

Ramsar sites are wetlands designated as being of international importance according to the Ramsar Convention on Wetlands. Traditionally, the importance of a site for breeding or visiting birds was a major consideration for designation.

ARUBA

The Bubali Pond IBA is a freshwater area, created by the effluent of a waste water facility. Over the years it has attracted many waterbirds. Remarkable is its roost of Neotropic Cormorants, but there are many more bird species. The Aruba government wanted to designate this area as a Ramsar site in the early 1980s, but because of bureaucratic problems that was never realised.

Tierra de Sol Saliña IBA is a natural wetland within the private property of a golf course frequented by waterbirds including Caribbean Coots and several species of ducks, but also shorebirds during migration. The saliña can dry out periodically.

The Oranjestad Reef Islands IBA and the San Nicolas Bay Reef islands IBA are important nesting areas for terns form April to August, at which time access should be restricted.

Spaans Lagoen (Ramsar site no. 198) is the first Ramsar site in the western hemisphere, as Aruba is alphabetically before Bonaire. It is the main mangrove area of Aruba.

Parke Nacional Arikok is a protected area of 32km^2 in the north-east. The two highest hills of the island are included in this park. It is representative of a good portion of the Aruban landscape, geology and biological diversity, including birds.

CURAÇAO

The north-east Curaçao parks and coast IBA stretches from the airport to the north point of Curaçao. It includes the St Christoffel Park, with the highest point on the island, and the Shete Boka park. Some waterholes in the Christoffel Park are regularly visited by many birds during the dry season.

Malpais-St Michiel IBA includes the Saliña of St Michiel, where a few hundred flamingos often forage, and the artificial freshwater pond of Malpais which attracts waterfowl; after a dry period the pond will dry out.

The Muizenberg IBA is another artificial freshwater pond, originally created to collect water for the refinery by damming in a run-off area. The water area is much larger than Malpais and water will remain for a longer time. When filled it is a breeding area for many Caribbean Coots, some Pied-billed Grebes and Black-bellied Whistling Ducks.

The Jan Thiel Lagoon IBA is a hypersaline lagoon with a rubble barrier closing it off from the sea; it is surrounded by woodlands. However, development is rapidly encroaching. On a small island and on the salt pond dykes Common and Least Terns breed from April to August and many shorebirds will use the shores during the autumn and spring migration. Up to a few hundred flamingos usually forage, except when the salinity drops because of rain. There is too much disturbance during the sensitive periods, and a strong management regime is warranted.

Klein Curaçao, an island about 10km south-east of Curaçao, is an IBA because Least Terns regularly breed there. Day-trips are organised, mainly for diving and the beach. Several seabirds can be seen as well as shorebirds like Ruddy Turnstones.

At Klein Hofje there is a water treatment plant, whose effluent basins are visited by many ducks, rails and cormorants all year round.

Several inner bays are fringed by mangroves, including the harbour. Many species of herons can be found there of which the most common, the Green Heron, is more easily heard than seen.

BONAIRE

Bonaire has two 'signature' bird species; the American Flamingo, for which it has the most consistent breeding colony in the southern Caribbean; and the Yellow-shouldered Parrot.

The Washington-Slagbaai National Park IBA in the north of the island covers about 20% of Bonaire and includes the highest hill on the island. It has a varied habitat for birds, including several saliñas and hypersaline inner bays separated from the sea by a rubble barrier, where flamingos remain the whole year: Bartol, Funchi, Slagbaai (Ramsar site no. 203) and Goto (Ramsar site no. 202). The water level in Saliña Mathijs can vary with the rains, but when it is full can host several hundred flamingos. There are also several large Yellow-shouldered Parrot roosts in the park. Pos Bronswinkel and Pos di Mangel are two freshwater pools in the park where, particularly in the dry season, birds congregate.

Dos Pos IBA is in the south-west of the park, east of Gotomeer, and includes wells with small fruit plantations, and also several cliff-surrounded valleys where the Yellow-shouldered Parrot roosts in some numbers. The area around the wells is used by several migrant warblers and other songbirds.

The Washikemba-Fontein-Onima IBA stretches along the northern and eastern coast. In the northern part there is the natural spring at Fontein and the pond at Onima. Parrots breed along the adjacent cliffs, and Least Terns nest on the coastal flat. Coots and other waterfowl congregate at the ponds of Onima and Washikemba, and several other species can also be seen, including at times flamingos.

Klein Bonaire is both an IBA and a Ramsar site (no. 201). This offshore island is important for the Caribbean Elaenia and as a breeding site for terns. The coral reefs surrounding the island are some of the most popular for diving.

Lac is also both an IBA and a Ramsar site (no. 199). It has the largest mangrove expanse of all three islands; but it also has extensive sea-grass beds, hypersaline waters and much more. Lac is a very dynamic area which is constantly changing, creating ever more diversity. In the open basin Brown Pelicans, Great Blue Herons, terns and other seabirds can be seen. Around the mangroves are other herons, Yellow Warblers and Brown-throated Parakeets. In the hypersaline areas in the north-east, hundreds of flamingos can be seen.

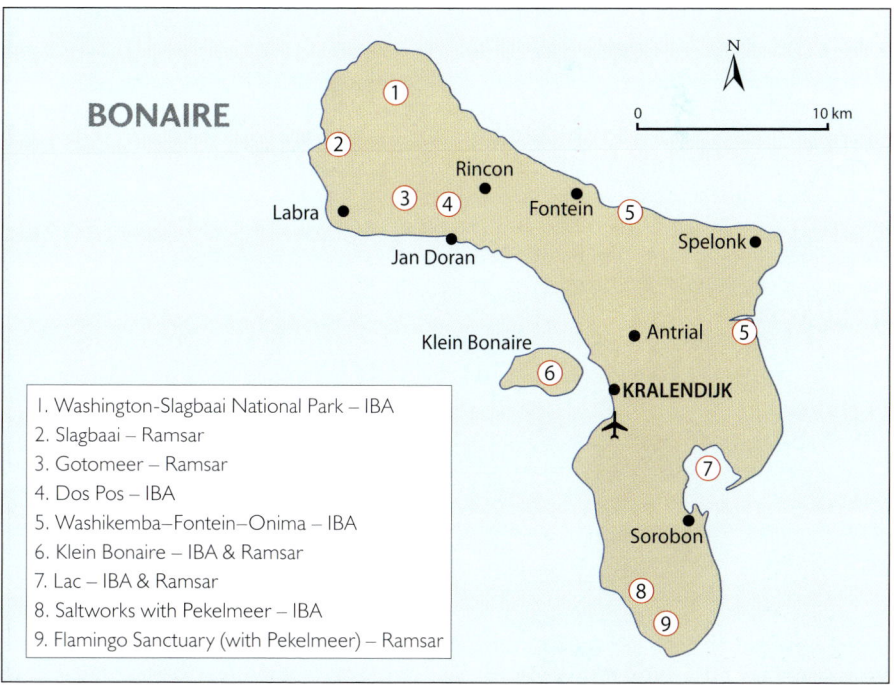

1. Washington-Slagbaai National Park – IBA
2. Slagbaai – Ramsar
3. Gotomeer – Ramsar
4. Dos Pos – IBA
5. Washikemba–Fontein–Onima – IBA
6. Klein Bonaire – IBA & Ramsar
7. Lac – IBA & Ramsar
8. Saltworks with Pekelmeer – IBA
9. Flamingo Sanctuary (with Pekelmeer) – Ramsar

Pekelmeer Saltworks forms an IBA with a Ramsar site (no. 200) within. When the salt works were re-established and extended in the 1960s, a flamingo sanctuary was enclosed on the eastern shores of the original Pekelmeer where the flamingos bred. This area is now protected and controlled by the salt facilities, not only for access, but the water is also kept at an optimal level. It is the most consistent flamingo breeding colony in the south Caribbean with up to 7000 adult birds during the breeding season. In the other ponds of the salt works, not only flamingos but also herons and many other birds can be seen. Within the salt works several tern species also breed.

CONSERVATION

Only two breeding species on the islands are considered threatened by the IUCN (International Union for Conservation of Nature) Red List (IUCN, 2010) – the Yellow-shouldered Parrot *(Amazona barbadensis,* VU) and the Caribbean Coot *(Fulica caribaea,* NT). All other species considered threatened by the IUCN are migrants or vagrants. However, the IUCN only assesses species, not subspecies, and the islands do hold populations of some threatened subspecies. They include the local subspecies of Barn Owl *(Tyto alba)* on Curaçao and Bonaire, and Burrowing Owl *(Athene cunicularia)* on Aruba.

Since 1926, bird protection laws have been in effect on the islands for certain species. The primary species initially thought to be in need of protection was the Troupial *Icterus icterus,* which in later years was shown to be quite common. The original list of protected species actually concentrated more on well-known rather than threatened species, although it later also protected the vulnerable Yellow-shouldered Parrot and several tern species.

In 1995 for Aruba and in 1998 for the other islands a new law was passed which directly applied the protection measures prescribed by several international treaties. The relevant treaties for bird protection were the Convention on the International Trade in Endangered Species of wild flora and fauna (CITES), the regional Special Protected Area and Wildlife Protocol (SPAW) of the Cartagena Convention, and the Convention on Migratory Species (CMS). The species on the lists of these treaties are appropriately protected, but only for Aruba are the species on Appendix II of CITES locally protected; for the other islands these species are only controlled in international trade. However, Bonaire also protects locally some species not listed by a treaty.

Besides the species protection, two treaties implemented by these laws and relevant to bird conservation are the Convention on Biological Diversity and the Ramsar Wetlands Convention. In 1980, when the Kingdom ratified the Ramsar convention, six wetlands of international importance were designated. These were the first six Ramsar sites in the Western Hemisphere; one on Aruba (Spaans Lagoen) and five on Bonaire (Slagbaai, Gotomeer, Klein Bonaire, Pekelmeer with the Flamingo Sanctuary, and Lac). Globally, there are now almost 2,000 Ramsar sites.

LOCAL NAMES

The local language on all three islands is Papiamento, a creole language derived originally from a pidgin Portuguese, but developed under the influence of Arawak, Spanish, Judeo-Spanish, Dutch, French, English and several African languages. Local bird names are often only generic, and even then show much variation between islands and (human) families. Also, although Papiamento is a language with a small speaker base, it has two official spellings.

In a recent checklist of the birds of Aruba, Curaçao and Bonaire (Prins *et al,* 2009), many local names for species were provided. We have chosen to give only some of the names, mainly to keep the text short. Some readers may therefore find that their favourite names are not included. If there would be a need for more standardised Papiamento names for birds, the linguists should first get together to establish a single spelling.

SPECIES ACCOUNTS

PLATE 1: BOBWHITE, COMB DUCK AND GOOSE

Crested Bobwhite *Colinus cristatus*   L 20cm
Ar Cocuí; **Bon** Not recorded; **Cur** Sloké; **NL** Kuifkwartel.
A small gamebird and quite difficult to observe. Looks like a very small partridge but more rounded. Brown, heavily speckled with white all over. Male has buff head with strong pattern of dark stripes, conspicuous crest. Female plainer with smaller crest; no dark face pattern. The birds on the islands belong to the nominate ssp. distinguished from others by longer crest, rufous throat with pale malar and ear-spots but sides of head darker. **Voice** Call melodious whistle *coo-kwee* with the second note inflected upward. It could be interpreted as 'bob-white'. More often heard than seen. In groups utters chirping and cheeping contact notes. **HH** Found in arid thorn and cactus shrub. Will go near houses where chickens are being fed. Mostly seen in pairs or as a family with small chicks walking in single file. **Status** Breeds on Aruba and Curaçao but not present on Bonaire.

Comb Duck *Sarkidiornis melanotos*   L 55cm (female) to 75cm (male)
Ar Pato bòlòbònchi; **Bon**, **Cur** Patu bòlòbònchi; **NL** Knobbeleend.
Very large duck with marked size difference between the sexes. Male immediately recognisable by large black comb at base of bill. Head and neck white with numerous black spots. A dark line descends from the crown along the back of the neck. Rest of body white. Back and wings black with strong blue-green metallic sheen. Female much smaller, lacks comb and head has more black spots. Immature body light brown with crown and upperparts dark brown; dark eyeline noticeable. **Voice** Silent on its wintering grounds. In breeding season may give hissing whistles and grunts. **HH** Bird of lakes and marshes. Shy and often in pairs. Grazes on land or takes vegetable matter from shallow waters. **Status** Rare visitor from South America. There are three records from Aruba, two records from Curaçao and two from Bonaire, all were made after heavy rains.

Greater White-fronted Goose *Anser albifrons*   L 75cm
Ar Ganso cara blanco; **Bon**, **Cur** Not recorded; **NL** Kolgans.
Immediately recognisable by size alone. Grey-brown goose with irregular black bars on belly. Pink bill and white patch on face encircling base of bill. Yellow feet. Immature lacks the black belly bars and the white face-patch, and has paler bill. **Voice** High-pitched yodeling sound. **HH** On lakes, ponds and in marshes in northern US and Canada. **Status** Recorded once on Aruba. Occurrence must be considered exceptional as it has not otherwise been recorded south of Cuba. Visitor from North America.

Crested Bobwhite

Comb Duck

Greater White-fronted Goose

PLATE 2: WHISTLING DUCKS

White-faced Whistling Duck *Dendrocygna viduata*   L 45cm
Ar Pato pigigi cara blanco; **Bon** Not recorded; **Cur** Patu pidjidji kara blanku; **NL** Witwangfluiteend.
Slightly smaller than other whistling ducks. Characteristic *white face* distinguishes it clearly from the other species. Rest of head and hindneck black. Body reddish-brown with barred underparts. Upperwing-coverts with light edges, giving a scaled appearance. Bill black, feet dark grey. Female a drabber version of the male with more extensive white on face and neck. In flight shows black wings and no white in tail. **Voice** A three-syllable soft whistle with emphasis on first syllable, given in flight or when disturbed. **HH** Usually in large flocks, often with Black-bellied Whistling Ducks. Feeds by day and night on vegetable matter in freshwater ponds. **Status** Rare visitor from South America. May show up on the islands after heavy rains but on Aruba only one record (single bird) and from Curaçao there are only two records: one of two birds and the other a group of 28. No records from Bonaire.

Black-bellied Whistling Duck *Dendrocygna autumnalis*   L 50cm
Ar Pato pigigi barica preto; **Bon**, **Cur** Patu pidjidji barika pretu; **NL** Zwartbuikfluiteend.
Immediately recognisable by *red bill and pink feet*. Mainly rusty brown with cheeks and foreneck grey. Wings black with large white shoulder patch, very conspicuous when bird is standing still. Belly black. Female has more white in face. Immature duller with greyish bill. Local ssp. is *D. a. discolor* from South America and West Indies. **Voice** Emits a clear hissing whistle during flight or when disturbed. **HH** Has established itself on islands after the creation of permanent freshwater ponds (Bubali pond on Aruba and Klein Hofje on Curaçao). Usually in large groups except when breeding when pairs look for suitable nesting sites. Will rest there during the day and fly to its feeding ground at night, when characteristic whistle may be heard overhead. Feeds on all kinds of vegetable matter in the water but also grazes on land. When heavy rains fill the many freshwater reservoirs, it will spread out over the islands. **Status** Breeds on Aruba and Curaçao. Rare visitor on Bonaire. Originally from South America.

Fulvous Whistling Duck *Dendrocygna bicolor*   L 50cm
Ar Pato pigigi kané; **Cur** Not recorded; **Bon** Patu podjidji kané; **NL** Rosse fluiteend.
Goose-like large duck with long legs and neck. Mainly rich cinnamon-brown with darker brown on top of the head and hindneck. Wings and back black scaled with buff. Elongated white flank feathers are edged black, forming black and white stripes when standing erect. White uppertail-coverts. *Bill and feet lead grey*. In flight wings are all black. **Voice** Emits a reedy whistle when flying. **HH** Usually travels in flocks, often mixed with Black-bellied Whistling Ducks. Feeds mainly at night on grass seeds and all vegetable matter in fresh water. In daytime rests in freshwater ponds. **Status** Rare visitor from South America. A group of four adult birds was observed on Aruba and also from Bonaire a group of four adults was reported. In South America the numbers of these birds have declined dramatically in recent years.

PLATE 3: DABBLING DUCKS I

Northern Shoveler *Anas clypeata* L 47cm
Ar Pato boca hancho; **Bon**, **Cur** Patu boka hanchu; **NL** Slobeend.
Characteristic feature is the *large wedge-shaped bill*. Male has green head and neck, white breast and chestnut-coloured sides and belly. White spot before the black tail. Female is mottled brown all over. Both sexes have *green speculum and large blue patch on wing*, clearly visible in flight. Feet yellowish. In flight the large bill is a distinguishing feature. **Voice** Silent on wintering grounds. Otherwise male a low *took-took-took*, female a hoarse quack. **HH** Most often seen in pairs or small groups. Dabbling duck which sifts the surface water for small invertebrates and vegetable matter. Mainly in fresh water but might be found in inner bays. **Status** Winter visitor from North America. Though observed regularly, never appears in large numbers.

Mallard *Anas platyrhynchos* L 55cm
Ar, **Cur** Not recorded; **Bon** Patu rabu di krùl; **NL** Wilde eend.
Male has shiny green head with narrow white ring around the neck. Breast chestnut, rest of plumage greyish except for the white tail. Yellow bill and orange feet. Female mottled brown all over, yellow bill may show some orange, orange feet and white tail. In flight both sexes show a *blue speculum bordered at both sides with white*. **Voice** Generally silent on wintering grounds. Otherwise utters familiar quacking call. **HH** Found at freshwater ponds and marshy areas where it will feed on all kinds of vegetable matter. **Status** Rare visitor from North America during northern winter. Known from three records, all adult females, from Bonaire.

American Wigeon *Anas americana* L 50cm
Ar Pato amerikana; **Bon**, **Cur** Patu merikano; **NL** Amerikaanse smient.
Large duck; male easily recognisable by white crown, giving it a 'bald' appearance. Green wedge behind the eye. Mainly grey-brown with a pinkish sheen. Round white spot in front of black tail. Female brown with grey head and neck. *Green speculum* clearly visible in both sexes. Bill lead grey. *White coverts form a line along the flanks and are very conspicuous in flight*. **Voice** Silent on wintering grounds. Otherwise the male has a three-syllable whistle *whee-whee-whee* with emphasis on second syllable. The female utters low grunting quacks. **HH** Occurs on marshland and shallow lakes. Feeds on all kinds of vegetable matter. **Status** Regular visitor, found on freshwater ponds in northern winter. The birds observed on the islands are migrants from North America.

Cinnamon Teal *Anas cyanoptera* L 40cm
Ar Pato koló kané; **Bon**, **Cur** Not recorded; **NL** Kaneeltaling.
Male in breeding plumage easily recognised by its reddish-chestnut colour. However, both sexes in winter plumage are difficult to distinguish from Blue-winged Teal in winter plumage as both show blue wing patch and green speculum in flight. Male Cinnamon Teal has yellow to red eyes and female has dark eyes. *Bill larger and more spatulate* than in Blue-winged Teal. Overall darker plumage and *never shows the white crescent in front of the eyes*. **Voice** Quite similar to Blue-winged Teal. Male a thin whistled *tsee-tsee*, female a high quack. **HH** Areas of shallow fresh water, streams and marshes. **Status** Rare winter visitor from North America. Only one record – an adult male on Aruba (Tierra del Sol).

26

PLATE 4: DABBLING DUCKS II

Green-winged Teal *Anas crecca* L 35cm
Ar Pato ala bèrdè; **Bon**, **Cur** Patu ala bèrdè; **NL** Wintertaling.
Smaller than Blue-winged Teal and more greyish with a brown head. Speculum is *deep green bordered by two white lines and shows as a dark patch in flight*. Conspicuous *vertical white stripe in front of the wing is characteristic*. Shows white belly in flight, Blue-winged shows dark belly. The birds encountered on the islands belong to the American ssp. *A. c. carolinensis*. **Voice** Male a short whistle, female a short quack. **HH** Normally a bird of marshes and rivers, it can be found on freshwater ponds with flocks of Blue-winged Teals. **Status** Rare winter visitor from North America. Only one record from Curaçao (Muizenbergdam) and two from Aruba (Bubali pond).

Blue-winged Teal *Anas discors* L 39cm
Ar Pato morèkè; **Bon**, **Cur** Patu morèkè; **NL** Blauwvleugeltaling.
Mainly brown, medium-sized duck. Male with grey head. *Blue patch on upper wing conspicuous especially in flight*. Green speculum. Feet and slender bill brown. In breeding plumage the male acquires a *white crescent in front of the eyes* and a round white spot in front of the black tail. Female brownish all over with black and white streaking. The birds staying on the islands during the northern winter are in non-breeding plumage when arriving in September but in December the males moult to breeding plumage. **Voice** Male a thin whistle, female a high quack. **HH** Found on freshwater ponds, where it dabbles for all kinds of vegetable matter. **Status** Regular winterer and non-breeding summer visitor. The birds on the islands are migrants from North America. However, a small number oversummer, at least on Curaçao at Klein Hofje. Matings have been observed but no breeding has been recorded.

Northern Pintail *Anas acuta* L 58cm
Ar Pato rabo largo; **Bon** Patu rabu largu; **Cur** Not recorded; **NL** Pijlstaart.
Long, slender, long-necked bird with the *typical pointed tails of pintails*, greatly lengthened in the male. Male with chocolate-brown head, white neck with white line running up to a point behind the eye. Upperparts and sides a finely mottled grey. *Conspicuous round white spot before the black tail*. Bill grey. Female mottled brown. In flight the green speculum bordered by a light line is visible in the male; much duller, almost non-existent in female. **Voice** Not often heard on wintering grounds. Male emits a two-syllable whistle, *prreep-prreep*, female a soft quack. **HH** Occurs in all types of wetlands, including brackish waters. **Status** Rare winter visitor from North America, only observed three times on Aruba and twice on Bonaire.

White-cheeked Pintail *Anas bahamensis* L 45cm
Ar Pato di aña; **Bon**, **Cur** Patu di aña; **NL** Bahamapijlstaart.
Immediately recognisable by *white cheeks and red bill-base*. White cheeks extend to throat. Mottled brown appearance with pointed tail, longer in male than in female. Bill tipped grey-blue and feet grey. Underparts speckled black. Green speculum conspicuous in both sexes. Local birds are of nominate ssp. from Caribbean and northern South America. **Voice** Mostly silent. Male may emit soft whistles, female a series of low quacks. **HH** Prefers fresh water but may be found in inner bays too. Always present on the freshwater ponds of Klein Hofje (Curaçao), Bubali (Aruba) and Playa Grande (Bonaire). In wet years will spread out over the islands. In the dry season large numbers may congregate in the few freshwater ponds that remain. Numbers fall in excessively dry years. **Status** Breeds throughout the year on all three islands.

PLATE 5: DIVING DUCKS

Masked Duck *Nomonyx dominicus* — L 35cm
Ar Not recorded; **Bon**, **Cur** Patu maskará; **NL** Maskerstekelstaart.
Small duck with characteristic **stiffened tail feathers, often pointed upward**. Male brown with black face and blue bill. White wingpatch clearly visible. Belly white. Female lighter brown with buff-coloured head, two black stripes across the head-sides. Eyes reddish, bill bluish-grey with black tip. **Voice** On wintering grounds a rolling *kirroo-kirroo*. **HH** Resembles a grebe in behaviour, sitting low in the water and diving to feed. Found on freshwater ponds after heavy rains. Mostly seen singly or in pairs. Will dive at the slightest sign of danger. **Status** Irregular visitor from South America during the dry season there.

Lesser Scaup *Aythya affinis* — L 43cm
Ar Pato tòper chikito; **Bon**, **Cur** Patu tòper chiki.; **NL** Kleine toppereend.
Resembles Ring-necked Duck but **back grey rather than black**. Male with head, neck, breast and tail black. Body finely streaked grey. Yellow eye. Bill bluish with no white rings. In winter plumage sides brown speckled with white, light ring at base of bill. Female uniformly brown with broad white ring at base of bill. Yellow eye. In flight both sexes show **broad white wingbar**. **Voice** Silent in winter. Otherwise male a low whistle, female a grating *garw-garw*. **HH** Marshes, lakes and ponds. Diving duck, sifting the bottom sediment for vegetable matter. Most often seen in pairs or small groups. **Status** Winter visitor from North America. Presence depends on availability of freshwater ponds. Usually arrives after significant rainfall.

Ring-necked Duck *Aythya collaris* — L 43cm
Ar Pato boca manchá; **Bon**, **Cur** Patu boka manchá; **NL** Ringsnaveleend.
Male strikingly black and white; head, neck, breast, back and tail black, sides very light grey with a conspicuous vertical white patch before the wing. White rings near the tip of the bill and at bill base. Yellow eye. Female almost uniformly brown with white eye-ring and a white streak behind the eye. White ring on bill before the head less clear than in male. Brown eye. In flight both sexes show a **broad grey wingbar**. **Voice** Silent in winter. Otherwise female has a grinding *keerrp-keerrp*. **HH** Found on freshwater lakes and ponds. In winter may visits bay. Dives to the bottom of the pond to sift the sediment for vegetable matter. **Status** Rare winter visitor from North America. One record from Aruba (Tierra del Sol), one from Bonaire (Washington-Slagbaai national park) and three from Curaçao (Muizenbergdam).

Bufflehead *Bucephala albeola* — L 35cm
Ar, **Bon** Not recorded; **Cur** Patu kabes di bagòn; **NL** Buffelkopeend.
Small duck, male striking white except for the head which is black with a large white patch breaking up the silhouette. Primaries black and with a black stripe over the back. Bill small, blue. Female upperparts dark brown and underparts lighter brown. White cheek-patch and white wingpatch. Bill brown. **Voice** Silent on wintering grounds. Otherwise male a long rolling note, female a loud quack. **HH** Lakes, ponds. On wintering grounds may be found in inner bays. **Status** Very rare winter visitor from North America. One record on the freshwater pond of Malpais (Curaçao).

PLATE 6: CORMORANTS AND PELICAN

Neotropic Cormorant *Phalacrocorax brasilianus*   L 64–70cm
Ar, **Bon**, **Cur** Deklá; **NL** Bigua aalscholver.
Slender bird with long neck, hooked bill and rather long wedge-shaped tail. Adult plumage black with green sheen. *Facial skin and gular pouch yellow to brown*, depending on season, with a narrow white line separating it from the head feathers. Bright blue-green eyes. Immature mostly all brown, lighter brown to almost white below. Local birds are of nominate ssp. from central and South America. **Voice** Mostly silent except for the occasional pig-like grunt. **HH** Can be found in inner bays resting among the mangroves or on any object sticking out of the water. Surface-dives for fish, using feet for propulsion underwater. **Status** Non-breeding resident on Bonaire and Curacao. Breeds on Aruba where nests have been reported from the Bubali pond.

Double-crested Cormorant *Phalacrocorax auritus*   L 80cm
Ar, **Cur** Not recorded; **Bon** Deklá orea; **NL** Geoorde aalscholver.
Resembles Neotropic Cormorant but much larger and more robust. Adult glossy black with *orange-yellow facial skin and gular pouch*. Small crest at either side of the head. No white line separating facial skin and head feathers. Immature dark brown with white sides of head, neck and breast though there is much variation in the amount of white. Gular pouch bright yellow. Also distinguishable by size alone from immature Neotropic Cormorant. **Voice** Mostly silent but gives occasional croaks and grunts. **HH** Coastal waters and inland lakes in North America south to the Bahamas and Cuba. **Status** Rare visitor. One record of an immature bird from Bonaire.

Brown Pelican *Pelicanus occidentalis*   L 114–140cm, W up to 200cm
Ar Ròganss; **Bon**, **Cur** Ganshi; **NL** Bruine pelikaan.
Massive, rather plump-looking bird; characteristic long bill with a large gular pouch. Adult has white head and neck, yellowish forehead and bluish-brown body. In breeding plumage hindneck a beautiful chestnut-brown. Immature head and neck brown, underparts a dirty-white. Southern Caribbean birds belong to nominate ssp.; bill shorter than 30cm which separates it from the longer-billed more northern *P. o. carolensis*, which has been recorded as winter visitor on the islands. Breeding has only been established with certainty on Aruba. **Voice** Occasionally gives a hoarse croak. **HH** Can be found all along the coast, preferring shallow waters. Plunge-dives to catch fish. Often roosts on piers or any object projecting from water. **Status** Non-breeding resident on Bonaire and Curacao. Breeding bird on Aruba.

PLATE 7: PETRELS AND SHEARWATERS

Black-capped Petrel *Pterodroma hasitata* L 40cm, W up to 100cm
Ar Parha di tormenta pèchi pretu; **Bon**, **Cur** Para di tormenta pèchi pretu; **NL** Zwartkapstormvogel.
In size intermediate between Audubon's and Great Shearwaters. Adult has *black cap with white forehead and neck*. Upperparts dark grey, underparts white with leading edge of underside of wing black. Characteristic *white uppertail-coverts*. Bill black and stubby. The alternation of black upperparts and white underparts when banking makes it very conspicuous, especially in the sunshine. **HH** Can only be observed at sea, where it glides low over the waves with stiff wings almost touching the water. Surface-feeds, mainly on squid, from the surface water. Is also active at dusk and night. **Status** Irregular visitor at sea.

Bulwer's Petrel *Bulweria bulwerii* L 28cm, W 55cm
Ar, **Bon**, Not recorded; **Cur** Para di tormenta Bulwer; **NL** Bulwer's stormvogel.
Small, slender petrel seen only at sea. Adult uniform sooty brown, long, narrow wings with *paler central wingbars* as only distinguishing feature. Relatively long, wedge-shaped tail. Black bill. **HH** Characteristic flight pattern, following straight course and banking sharply on stiff wings. Does not follow ships and feeds mainly at night when it will drift on the water and pick at fish, squid and plankton. **Status** Rare visitor at sea. Only observed once in territorial waters near Klein Curaçao but more observations from international waters north of the islands.

Audubon's Shearwater *Puffinus lherminieri* L 30cm, W 67cm
Ar Not recorded; **Bon**, **Cur** Kapiadó Audubon; **NL** Audubon's pijlstormvogel.
Uniform dark brown above, dark cap reaches below eye. White below, separation between dark and white very sharp. *Undertail-coverts dusky brown*. Bill brown, slender, relatively long and with upturned nose tubes. Local birds are of nominate ssp.; *P. l. loyemilleri* (defined by all-white underwing-coverts and no dark leading edge on wings) could occur here but no records so far. **HH** Flight characteristically alternates gliding with rapid wingbeats. Does not follow ships. Feeds while drifting on the water but also plunge-dives. **Status** Possible breeding bird. Thought to be nesting on Bonaire as pairs have been observed at cliff holes during breeding season but the presence of eggs could not be established. Most commonly seen at sea between Curaçao and Bonaire and around Klein Curaçao. Occasionally can be seen from the coast at the windwards sides of the islands.

Great Shearwater *Puffinus gravis* L 45–50cm, W 115cm
Ar, **Cur** Not recorded; **Bon** Kapiadó grandi; **NL** Grote pijlstormvogel.
Dark brown above and white below with a brown patch on the belly and dark bars on the underwings. Characteristic *black cap, white neck and white uppertail-coverts*. Strong hooked black bill. **Voice** Flocks give raw screeching similar to fighting cats. **HH** Flight fast and swooping, following straight course and often following ships in large flocks. Plunge-dives to catch its prey, often feeds on offal thrown from fishing boats. **Status** Rare visitor at sea. One carcass found on Bonaire. Bird of the Atlantic ocean and found only as dead birds washed ashore in different parts of the Caribbean.

Wilson's Storm-petrel *Oceanites oceanicus* L 18cm, W 40cm
Ar Parha di tormenta Wilson; **Bon**, **Cur** Para di tormenta Wilson; **NL** Wilson's stormvogeltje.
Blackish-brown all over with a conspicuous *crescent-shaped white rump-patch*, also visible from the side. The feet extend beyond the tail's edge in flight. *Tail not forked but square*, which distinguishes it from Leach's Storm-petrel. Bill black with tube-shaped nostrils. Whitish band across the upper wing coverts. **HH** Characteristically 'walks' on water, pattering lowered feet on surface, and often follows in the wake of a ship. **Status** Irregular visitor at sea. Most often observed by fishermen out at sea during the dolphinfish season. May be spotted from shore as sometimes follows ships into the harbour.

Leach's Storm-petrel *Oceanodroma leucorhoa* L 21cm, W 47cm
Ar Not recorded; **Bon**, **Cur** Para di tormenta Leach; **NL** Vaal stormvogeltje.
Rare visitor at sea. Looks very much like Wilson's Storm-petrel but is *paler brown, wing band more conspicuous, white rump patch is narrower with a median grey line and does not run as far underneath the tail. Tail is more forked*. In flight the feet do not extend beyond the tail's edge. Local birds belong to nominate ssp. **Voice** High hooting sounds at night in flight. **HH** Does not follow ships. Flight erratic, changing direction and speed rapidly and even showing vertical jumps. Does not 'walk' on the water. May follow fishing boats to find offal but will not follow other ships. **Status** Rare visitor at sea. Has been seen from shore on Bonaire and Curaçao. Can be seen at sea but mainly in eastern Caribbean during the northern winter.

PLATE 8: TROPICBIRDS AND FLAMINGO

White-tailed Tropicbird *Phaethon lepturus* L 40cm (excl. central tail feathers), W 92cm
Ar Not recorded; **Bon**, **Cur** Bubi rabu largu blanku.; **NL** Witstaartkeerkringvogel.
Very much like Red-billed Tropicbird, also with elongated central tail feathers which double the bird's length. Smaller than Red-billed, with **conspicuous black band across the upperside of the wing**. **No grey stripes on back**. **Black stripe runs from bill-base but ends immediately behind the eye**. Bill colour, in spite of the bird's name, varies from red to blackish. Imm with yellow bill and except for size, almost identical to immature Red-billed Tropicbird but less barring and no black tail-tips. The birds recorded belong to *P. l. catesbyi* from the Caribbean. **Voice** Harsh screeches and staccato notes. **HH** Pelagic in habits and, like Red-billed Tropicbird, mostly seen in pairs. **Status** Rare visitor at sea. Only observed a few times north of Bonaire and Curaçao. [Alt: Yellow-billed Tropicbird]

Red-billed Tropicbird *Phaethon aethereus* L 50–60cm (excl. central tail feathers), W 100cm
Ar Not recorded; **Bon**, **Cur** Bubi rabu largu shouru; **NL** Roodsnavelkeerkringvogel.
Dazzlingly white bird. Central tail feathers fine and greatly elongated, adding another 50cm to the bird's length. Wingtips black and on the back a **pattern of grey lines**. **Black line runs from bill-base to beyond eye**. Bill bright red. Immature yellow bill which may lead to confusion with Yellow-billed Tropicbird; Red-billed immature more heavily barred, tail feathers have black tips. Immature lacks elongated tail feathers. Local birds belong to ssp. *P. a. mesonauta* from the Caribbean and east Pacific. **Voice** Makes a whistling sound as it flies past. Loud screeches on breeding grounds. **HH** Very pelagic, only comes to land to breed. Nearest known breeding site is on Los Roques and Los Hermanos (Venezuela). **Status** Irregular visitor at sea. Nine records from Bonaire and Curaçao, including dead birds washed ashore. Only two sightings from coastline. Fishermen have a local name for the bird, indicating they see it regularly at sea.

American Flamingo *Phoenicopterus ruber* L 140–175cm
Ar, **Cur** Flamingo; **Bon** Chogogo; **NL** Rode flamingo.
Intensely pink to almost red-coloured. Unmistakable with its long neck, heavy, bent bill and long pink legs. Wingtips black. Immature grey with upperparts and flight feathers brown, slowly attaining pink adult coloration. Male larger than female, obvious when pair marches with stretched necks during courtship. Local birds are of the nominate ssp. from the Caribbean. **Voice** A goose-like *gobbledy-gook* giving rise to its local name of *chogogo*. Trumpeting sounds during courtship. **HH** Shallow waters such as salt pans, freshwater ponds and inner bays where it sifts the water and bottom sediment for various invertebrates and vegetable matter. During the breeding season makes daily foraging flights to the coastal area of Venezuela. **Status** Breeding colony in Bonaire's salt works is the largest in the whole southern Caribbean population. A smaller population nests near Los Olivitos, Venezuela. Unsuccessful breeding attempts known from Curaçao. Common visitor to Curaçao, occasional on Aruba (except for semi-captives on some hotel grounds). [Alt: Caribbean Flamingo]

PLATE 9: FRIGATEBIRDS

Magnificent Frigatebird *Fregata magnificens*   L 97–107cm, W up to 225cm

Ar Makuaku; **Bon** Maniwá; **Cur** Skèrchi; **NL** Amerikaanse fregatvogel.
Unmistakable anchor-like silhouette with scissor-like tail, long hooked beak and prominently angled wings, which may show a shiny band. Adult male **all black** with red throat pouch, inflated in display at the start of the breeding season (October). Female with white chest and blue eye-ring. Immature white to buff head and white chest. **Voice** Vocal only when in colonies, making hoarse rattling noises. **HH** Very adept at picking fish from surface, which may involve amazing aerial acrobatics. Chases after other fish-eating birds to steal their prey from them. **Status** Non-breeding resident. Can be seen all along the coast and at sea. Rests in mangroves or on steep cliffs. Occasional nesting suspected on islands in Paardenbaai on Aruba but never positively confirmed.

Great Frigatebird *Fregata minor*   L 85–105 cm, W up to 230cm

Ar Makuaku menor; **Bon**, **Cur** Not recorded; **NL** Grote fregatvogel.
Resembles Magnificent Frigatebird. Male all-black with **shiny purple-green scapulars, almost forming a band across the wings when in flight**. Greyish scaling on axillaries. Female black with white throat and chest and conspicuous **red eye-ring**, clearly visible in flight. Subadult female with white patch on belly, black band across the chest. Juvenile with white head, throat and chest but **head and throat rust-tinged**. Subadult male has inverted white crescent on breast. **Voice** A gobbling turkey-like sound. **HH** Similar habits as Magnificent Frigatebird but less piratic. **Status** Rare visitor from tropical and subtropical Pacific and Western Atlantic ocean. One record of a subadult female from Aruba – the only record from the Caribbean.

PLATE 10: BOOBIES

Brown Booby *Sula leucogaster* — L 75cm, W 145cm
Ar, **Bon**, **Cur** Bubi brùin; **NL** Bruine gent.
Medium-sized bird mostly seen at sea or along the coast. Adult *brown with white belly sharply separated from brown chest*. Large pointed yellowish-pink bill and yellowish feet. Broad white line on underside of wing. Tail wedge-shaped. Immature brown with lighter belly. Belongs to *S. l. leucogaster* from the Caribbean. **Voice** Silent in flight. Near nests the usual repertoire of hisses, whistles and grunts. **HH** Usually skims the waves to dive at shallow angle when prey is seen. Stays closer to shore than other boobies, so is observed more often. **Status** Non-breeding resident and rather common on all three islands. Rests on rocks near the shore at fixed roosting sites including Malmok on Bonaire and Watamula on Curaçao. May visit piers or buoys for short rests. No breeding has been reported from the islands.

Masked Booby *Sula dactylatra* — L 80cm, W 165cm
Ar Bubi blanco; **Bon**, **Cur** Bubi blanku; **NL** Maskergent.
Largest booby in the area. Adult white with strongly contrasting black flight feathers. Long pointed yellowish bill and yellowish feet. Pointed *black tail*. Bare facial skin dark giving masked appearance. Immature brown above with conspicuous white ring around hindneck. Belly white. White edges of feathers on upperparts give it a barred appearance not seen in other boobies. Belongs to *S. d. dactylatra* from the Caribbean. **Voice** Silent in flight. Hisses, whistles and grunts near nest. **HH** Feeds at open sea, most pelagic of the boobies. Plunge-dives to catch fish and squid. **Status** Rare visitor. Only a few exhausted birds have been found on Bonaire and Aruba. Two sightings off the coast of Bonaire.

Red-footed Booby *Sula sula* — L 70cm, W 145cm
Ar Bubi pia còrá; **Bon**, **Cur** Bubi pia kòrá; **NL** Roodpootgent.
Smallest of the boobies that can be seen in the Caribbean. Very variable in colour pattern. White tail is diagnostic in most morphs. Brown morph: light brown all over or with white tail, rump and lower belly. White morph: like Masked Booby but may show a *completely white tail*. Dark carpal patch on the underside of wing. In both morphs adult has a blue-grey bill, thinner than in the other two booby species. Immature completely brown with greyish bill. No sharp division between belly and chest coloration. Caribbean race is the nominate. **Voice** Silent in flight. Near nests a series of hisses, whistles and grunts. **HH** Sometimes seen with Brown Boobies at their roosting sites. Mostly seen at sea, especially at the northern and southern capes of Bonaire and Curaçao. Follows schools of predatory fish chasing schools of smaller fish. Plunge-dives for fish. **Status** Non-breeding visitor.

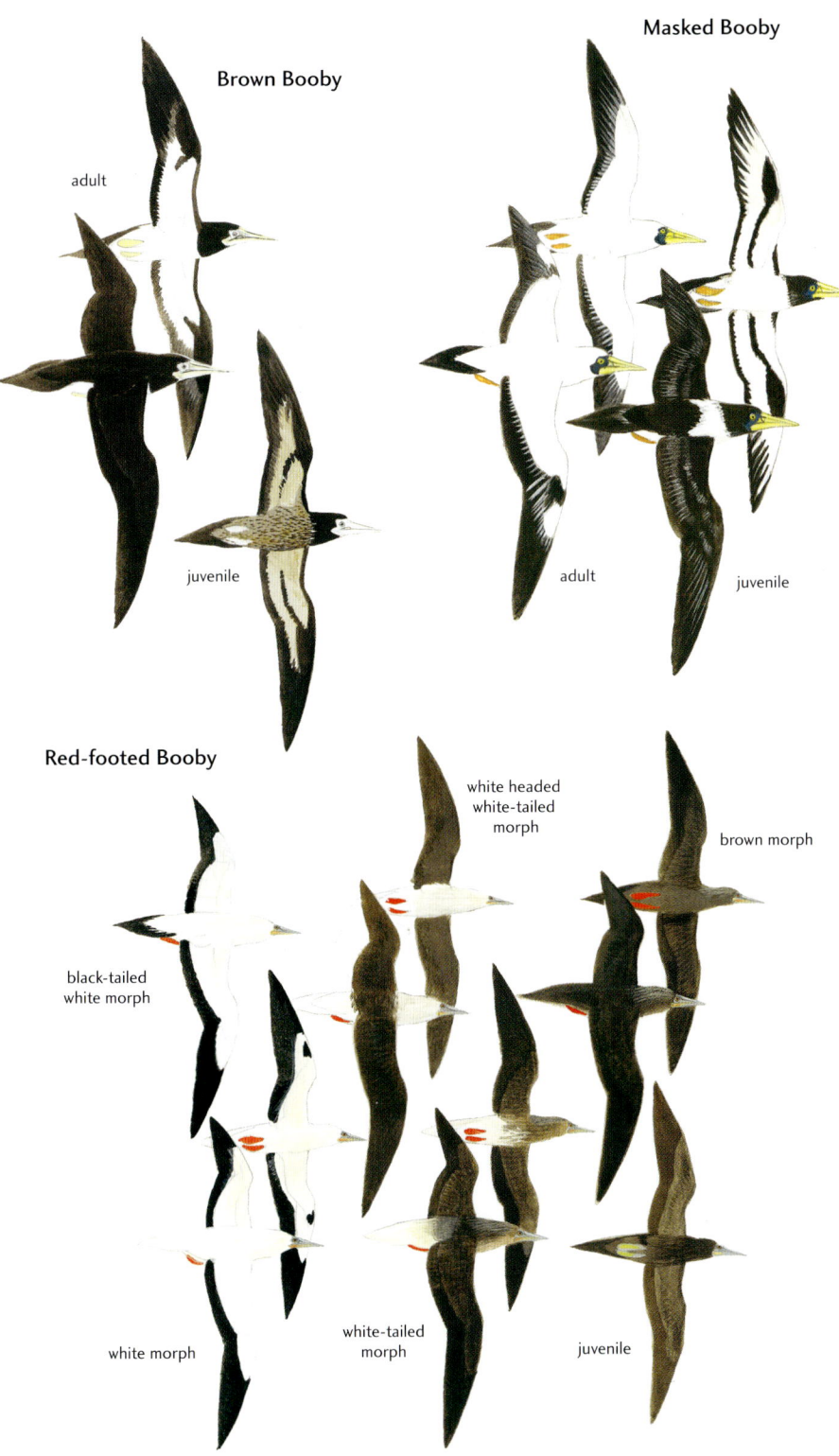

PLATE 11 : BITTERNS AND HERONS

Least Bittern *Ixobrychus exilis* L 27cm
Ar, **Bon** Not recorded; **Cur** Garabèt enano; **NL** Zuid-Amerikaanse Woudaap.
Small egret-like bird coloured in delicate shades of rufous and buff. Male has black crown connected by a black line on the neck to black back and tail with two conspicuous buff stripes on shoulders. Underparts buff, flight feathers and hindneck and sides of neck rufous. Yellowish bill and legs. Yellow eyes. In female black replaced by dark brown and lacks black line on neck. Immature scaled above and streaked below. **Voice** Low grunts and a booming call. **HH** Bird of swamps where it will remain motionless between the reeds in upright position. When disturbed flies away wildly before suddenly dropping down again. Usually solitary and feeds mainly at dawn and dusk on fish, frogs, insects. **Status** Rare visitor from South America. One record from Curaçao (Muizenbergdam).

Pinnated Bittern *Botaurus pinnatus* L 65–75 cm
Ar Garabèt di caña.; **Bon**, **Cur** Not recorded; **NL** Zuid-Amerikaanse roerdomp.
Easily distinguished from other heron-like birds by its size and the **heavily mottled brown appearance**. Back is streaked brown, forehead brown with sides and back of neck buff, finely barred with black. The blackish flight feathers stand out in flight. Bill yellow and legs greenish-yellow. Orange eyes. Immature has streaked wings and back. **Voice** A loud booming *ooh-gachoonk*. **HH** Hides in tall vegetation alongside freshwater ponds. When discovered freezes in upright position, bill pointing up. Active mainly at night. **Status** Rare visitor from South America. One record from Aruba, a straggler caught in Oranjestad.

Green Heron *Butorides virescens* L 45–50cm, W 60cm
Ar, **Bon**, **Cur** Galiña di awa; **NL** Groene reiger.
Small secretive bird, hunched appearance makes it look smaller than it actually is. Wings bluish, **sides of neck chestnut-brown** bordering a white line on the foreneck, throat and breast striped. Striated Heron has grey sides of head and neck. Bill sturdy, black. Legs, feet and facial skin in front of eyes greenish-yellow. Immature brown with heavily streaked neck and underparts. Wings with more white lines than adult. Resident birds on the islands belong to the ssp. *B. v. maculata* which is smaller than the North American nominate. The latter may visit the islands but probably overlooked as the only difference is size. **Voice** Silent, but utters a hoarse shriek when disturbed. **HH** Secretive, skulking along the edges of inner bays and reluctant to take flight. Often perches on a low branch from which it may forage. Does not wade in water like other herons. **Status** Breeding bird. Breeds throughout the year on all three islands. Nest well hidden in thick bush or mangrove growth.

Striated Heron *Butorides striata* L 40cm, W 55cm
Ar Not recorded; **Bon**, **Cur** Galiña di awa strepiá; **NL** Mangrovereiger.
Very much like Green Heron but **sides of the head, neck and breast are grey not chestnut-brown**. Immature practically indistinguishable from immature Green Heron, except for **greyer neck and sides of head**. Bill yellow with black tip. Loral skin, legs and feet yellow. Formerly considered conspecific with Green Heron, and hybridisation has been reported from Trinidad and Tobago. Local birds are of nominate ssp. **Voice** Silent but when disturbed will give a loud *keoop*. **HH** Found on shores of freshwater ponds but also in salt pans and inner bays. Secretive habits like Green Heron. **Status** Rare visitor from South America, known from four records on Bonaire (near Pekelmeer) and one on Curaçao (Malpais). May easily be overlooked, due to similarity to Green Heron.

Great Blue Heron *Ardea herodias* L 110–130cm, W 175cm
Ar, **Bon**, **Cur** Garsa blou grandi; **NL** Amerikaanse blauwe reiger.
Blue-grey with white head and throat. Dark band runs from behind eye and extends in longer feathers behind the head. Long pointed **yellow bill and yellow legs**. Thighs chestnut. Immature with black crown, sides of head whitish and dark streaking on foreneck; bill mainly blackish. These birds belong to the rather small and pale grey nominate ssp. from North America. White morph completely white, resembling Great Egret, but size, strong bill and yellow legs are distinguishing features. An intermediate morph is mottled white and grey with white head and no dark band across the eye. The white and intermediate morphs are thought to belong to the South Caribbean race *A. h. repens*. **Voice** Mostly silent. When disturbed will utter a hoarse croak. **HH** Solitary, found in freshwater ponds, salt pans and inner bays. Wary, will take wing at the slightest disturbance. **Status** Regular visitor. Can be found on all three islands throughout the year.

PLATE 12: EGRETS

Cattle Egret *Bubulcus ibis* — L 50cm, W 60cm
Ar Garabèt di baca; **Bon**, **Cur** Garabèt di baka; **NL** Koereiger.
Looks small and compact as it almost always moves in a hunched position with neck withdrawn. Completely white with *thick, rather short yellow bill, yellow eyes and greenish-yellow legs*. In breeding plumage the bill and legs turn orange-red and the bird will show orange-brown feathers on its head, breast and wings. Immature distinguished by black legs. Local birds are of nominate ssp. **Voice** Mostly silent except for some croaking calls in roosting colonies and during courtship. **HH** More often on dry land than near water, chasing after insects. Follows goats and other cattle to pick up disturbed insects. At dusk will gather in roosting colonies, preferably isolated trees near water. **Status** Breeding bird. Will nest in mixed colonies together with Tricoloured Heron and Snowy Egret. Breeds on Aruba and Curaçao but is an irregular visitor to Bonaire.

Snowy Egret *Egretta thula* — L 50–60cm, W 95cm
Ar Garsa blanco chikito; **Bon**, **Cur** Garsa blanku chiki; **NL** Amerikaanse kleine zilverreiger.
Medium-sized white heron. *Black bill and legs but starkly contrasting yellow feet* were a distinguishing characteristic until the arrival of Little Egret. *Facial skin before the eye yellow*, which sets it apart from Little Egret in non-breeding plumage. In breeding plumage shows various long filamentous feathers on head and lower neck, and lace-like feathers on the scapular region, giving the bird a very elegant appearance. Immature with legs more greenish-yellow. Local birds are of the nominate ssp. **Voice** Mostly silent but may emit raucous calls. Soft *wark-wark* contact notes have been reported. **HH** Present throughout the year in freshwater ponds, inner bays, salt pans and along the coast in shallow water. Breeds among the mangroves but also in Calabash trees. **Status** Breeding bird, breeds on all three islands. In northern winter visitors from North America probably also encountered.

Little Egret *Egretta garzetta* — L 50–60cm, W 95cm
Ar Garsa blanco oropeo; **Bon**, **Cur** Not recorded; **NL** Kleine zilverreiger.
A recent arrival to the Caribbean area from Africa and Eurasia, seems to be expanding its range quickly. Like Snowy Egret but with *facial skin and lores bluish-grey*. In breeding plumage this changes to yellowish-orange; *only two* long plumes on head. No plumes on scapular region. There exists a dark morph which is grey all over except (in some) a white chin and throat. In this plumage it is quite similar to another new arrival to the area, the Western Reef Heron, which also occurs in a white morph. **Voice** Mostly silent but may give short grunts. In breeding colony (only breeding site in Caribbean recorded on Barbados so far) quite noisy with hisses, croaks and grunts. **HH** Very similar to Snowy Egret. Will visit freshwater ponds, salt pans and shallow inner bays. **Status** Rare visitor. Two records from Aruba (Tierra del Sol and Bubali pond). However, may be overlooked due to its similarity with the other two species mentioned above.

Great Egret *Ardea alba* — L 100cm, W 150cm
Ar Garsa blanca grandi; **Bon**, **Cur** Garsa blanku grandi; **NL** Grote zilverreiger.
All-white with long *yellow bill* and long *black legs and feet*. Eyes yellow though turn reddish during a short period in the breeding season. In breeding plumage shows elongated plumes hanging down from the scapular feathers. Size and the combination of black legs and yellow bill distinguish this bird from other white herons. Local birds belong to the American ssp. *A. a. egretta*. **Voice** Mostly silent but utters a loud, annoyed croak when flushed. **HH** Found on freshwater ponds but also in lagoons, inner bays and salt pans. Does not actively pursue prey but will stand still, waiting for fish or large aquatic insect larvae to venture close enough to strike. Often rests in mangroves together with other herons. **Status** Regular visitor from South America and may be found throughout the year. One possible breeding record from Klein Bonaire.

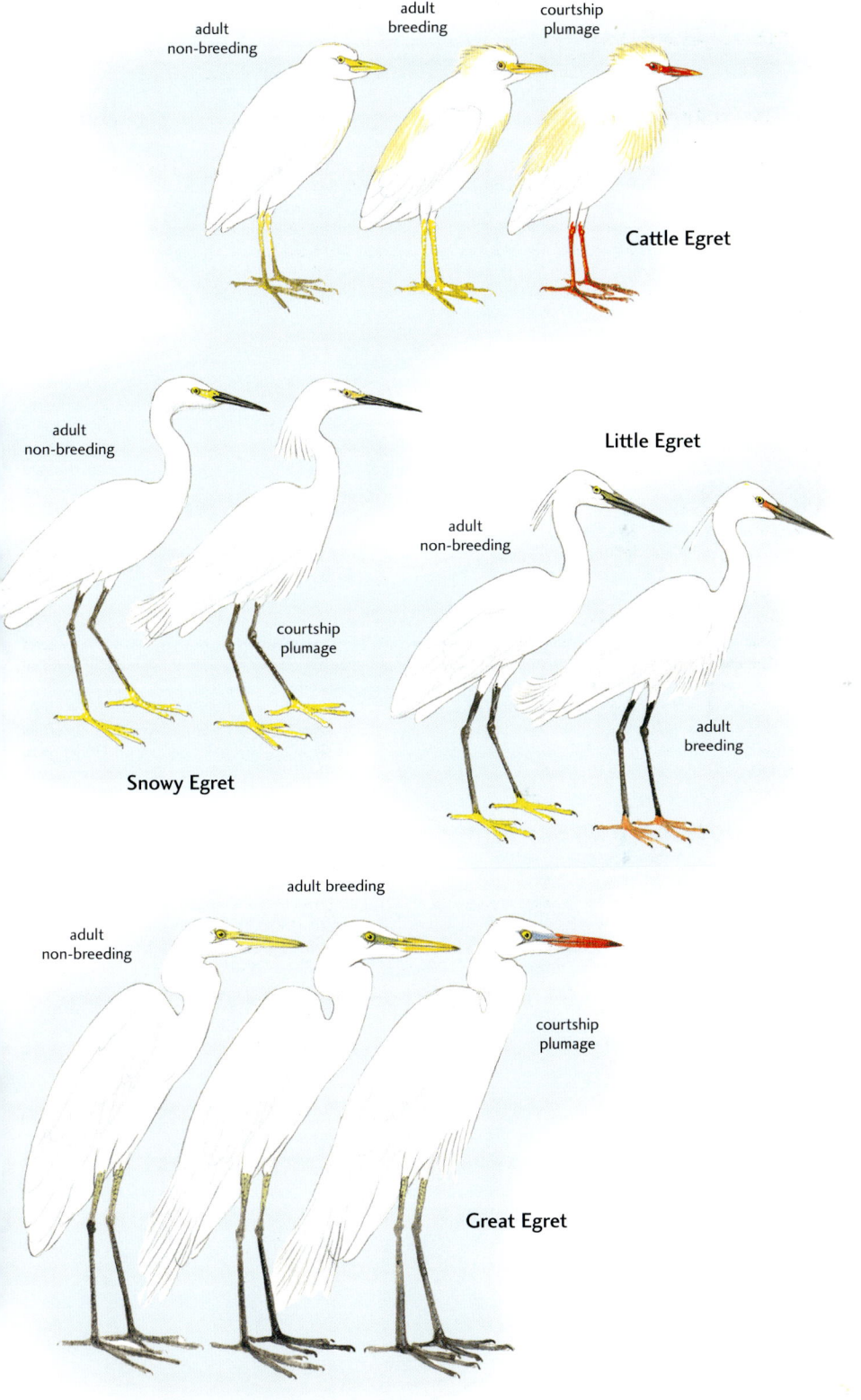

PLATE 13: EGRETS AND HERONS

Reddish Egret *Egretta rufescens* L 75–80cm, W 120cm
Ar Garsa corá; **Bon**, **Cur** Garsa korá; **NL** Roodhalsreiger.
Untidy-looking bird due to the impression of ruffled feathers on neck and breast. Adult slate grey with reddish head and neck. *Bill pinkish at base and black at the tip. Legs and feet grey bluish.* White morph completely white but can be distinguished from other white herons by bi-coloured bill and grey-blue legs. Intermediate morph is very rare. Immature of dark morph greyish with brownish head and neck. Imm of white morph has blackish bill. Local birds are of nominate ssp. from the Caribbean. **Voice** Mainly silent but soft grunts may be heard. **HH** Can be found in lagoons, salt pans, inner bays and on the reef wall. While hunting it may spread its wings, forming an umbrella of shade which attracts fish. **Status** Regular visitor and breeding bird. Breeding has been reported only from Bonaire. Visitors come from Caribbean region.

Tricoloured Heron *Egretta tricolor* L 65cm, W 95cm
Ar Garsa barica blanco; **Bon**, **Cur** Garsa bariku blanku; **NL** Witbuikreiger.
Slender medium-sized heron with long neck. *Grey-blue upper body with white belly and rump and reddish-brown breast and sides of neck.* A white line runs along the foreneck. Bill very long, bluish-grey, darker at tip. Legs greenish-yellow, changing to dull orange when breeding. In breeding plumage sports elongated white feathers from head and lace-like reddish-grey plumes from the back. Immature dark grey to brownish, duller than adult. Birds on the islands belong to the ssp. *E. t. ruficollis* from North America and the Caribbean, distinguished from the South American nominate by white line along the foreneck. **Voice** Mainly silent but will emit raucous alarm calls. Also quite noisy in courtship. **HH** Inhabits lagoons, salt pans, inner bays. May chase actively after prey in shallow water but in deeper water will wait for prey to come close. **Status** Breeding bird. Will nest in mangroves where it may mix with Snowy Egrets.

Little Blue Heron *Egretta caerulea* L 60–65cm, W 100cm
Ar Garsa blou chikito; **Bon**, **Cur** Garsa blou chikí; **NL** Kleine blauwe reiger.
Very dark blue, almost blackish all over, head and neck maroon with a purplish sheen. *Bicoloured bill with base grey blue and rest of bill black.* Legs and feet greenish. Iris yellow. Juvenile completely white but bicoloured bill distinguishes it from most other white herons. White morph of Reddish Egret has basal part of bill pinkish. As immature matures, passes through an intermediate phase with a mottled white-dark blue appearance. In breeding plumage shows elongated plumes on head, neck and back. **Voice** Mostly silent but may give loud raucous calls, similar to those heard from Snowy Egret. **HH** Found throughout the year in freshwater ponds, shallow bays, tidal lagoons and salt pans. Often stands motionless waiting for prey to come close. Also wades in a quite deliberate manner in shallow water or over rocks and mud. **Status** Regular visitor and irregular breeding bird. Breeding has been reported from Aruba and Bonaire. Visitor from both North and South America.

Whistling Heron *Syrigma sibilatrix* L 55cm, W 70cm
Ar, **Cur** Not recorded; **Bon** Garsa fluitdó; **NL** Fluitreiger.
Most colourful heron observed on the islands. Back grey, belly, lower back and rump white. Sides of head, neck, breast and front part of wings creamy. Rest of wings greyish-blue. Thick bill pink tipped black. Facial skin in front of and around eye bright blue. Legs greenish. Immature grey with white belly, rump and tail. **Voice** In flight often utters a thin whistle. **HH** Normally bird of flooded grasslands. On the islands visits shallow freshwater ponds and salt pans. **Status** Rare visitor from South America. One record on Bonaire (salt pans of Slagbaai).

PLATE 14: NIGHT HERONS AND GREBES

Boat-billed Heron *Cochlearius cochlearius*   L 55cm, W 90cm
Ar, **Cur** Not recorded; **Bon** Garabèt bok'i lancha; **NL** Schuitbekreiger.
Very much like Black-crowned Night Heron but with a *huge broad bill*. Black crown and nape. Wings and breast white, belly chestnut-brown. Flanks and underwing-coverts black, which makes it easily identifiable in flight. Immature pale brown above with brown turning to white on belly. **Voice** When feeding, low grunting *gook*. Has a song *oon-oonah-aan* mainly heard in breeding season. **HH** Visits freshwater ponds but also salt pans. **Status** Rare visitor from South America. One record on Bonaire (salt works).

Black-crowned Night Heron *Nycticorax nycticorax*   L 63–69cm, W 100cm
Ar Krabèchi bachi preto; **Bon**, **Cur** Krabèchi bachi pretu; **NL** Kwak.
Has hunch-backed appearance as it always perches with neck withdrawn, head almost between the wings. *Black back and crown, wings light grey and underparts white. Eyes red, bill black, feet greenish-yellow*. In breeding plumage has two elongated feathers from the back of the head. Immature streaked brown and white all over with greenish legs and greenish-yellow bill. Breeding population belongs to *N. n. hoactli* from northern South America and nearby islands. **Voice** When disturbed a harsh *kwark*. **HH** Occurs in freshwater ponds but also in lagoons and inner bays. Roosts by day and becomes active at night. Main food is fish but takes a large variety of aquatic animals. **Status** Since the establishment of permanent freshwater basins, breeds regularly near these. Breeding recorded from all three islands.

Yellow-crowned Night Heron *Nyctinassa violaceus*   L 70cm, W 110 cm
Ar, **Bon**, **Cur** Krabèchi; **NL** Geelkruinkwak.
Same posture as Black-crowned Night Heron but larger. Black head with *white crown* and white cheeks. Rest of body bluish-grey with strong striations on wings. Eye black with red iris. Bill black and feet yellow. In breeding plumage has crest of light yellow feathers bordered by black ones. Immature like immature Black-crowned but with *finer spots, more sharply defined. Legs more yellowish*. Local birds belong to *N. v. bancrofti* from Central America and West Indies. **Voice** When disturbed utters an indignant *kwok-kwok*, less harsh than Black-crowned Night Heron. **HH** Feeds at night and spends the day resting at the borders of freshwater ponds, in mangroves or under overhanging rocks near lagoons. Occasionally may be observed wading in the water in daytime. Feeds on crabs but will also take fish, and on land takes lizards and large insects. **Status** Breeding bird. Breeding recorded from Bonaire and Curaçao. No confirmed breeding on Aruba so far but probably nests in the vegetation near the Bubali pond.

Least Grebe *Tachybaptus dominicus*   L 20cm, W 127cm
Ar Zambuyadó chikito; **Bon**, **Cur** Sambuyadó chiki; **NL** Amerikaanse dodaars
Small, dark roundish bird with no visible tail and a pointed dark bill with a white tip. Very conspicuous *yellow-orange eyes*. Adult crown black, sides of head and neck more greyish, throat black, rest of body greyish-brown with underparts white mottled with brown. Non-breeding adult and immature plumage browner and more plain throughout. In flight shows large white areas on secondary flight feathers and long trailing feet. Subspecies present in area is *T. d. brachyrhynchus*. **Voice** Territorial adult makes loud rattling noise. **HH** Can be seen on any body of fresh water. May be absent during dry periods but appears with the first rains. Feeds underwater on insect larvae and small fish. **Status** Breeds on all three islands.

Pied-billed Grebe *Podilymbus podiceps*   L 33cm
Ar Zambuyadó pico diki; **Bon**, **Cur** Sambuyadó pik diki; **NL** Dikbekfuut
Larger and more robust than Least Grebe but similar in shape. *Thick, chicken-like bill with dark band near the tip*. Adult black throat and forehead, greyish sides of head and neck, rest of body grey-brown. White undertail-coverts conspicuous. Non-breeding adult and immature plain brown with white chin and throat, no dark band across bill. Young birds have striped heads. The resident birds belong to the ssp. *P. p. antarcticus*. Migrant *P. p. podiceps* from North and Middle America or *P. p. antillarum* from the Greater and Lesser Antilles may occur but no records so far. Both ssps are smaller and paler than *P. p. antarcticus*. **Voice** Seldom heard but said to make cuckoo-like noises. **HH** Freshwater ponds, sometimes in inner bays; needs more space than Least Grebe. May swim low in water with only head visible. Feeds underwater on small fish, crustaceans and insects. Very awkward on land; almost never leaves the water. **Status** Breeds on all three islands.

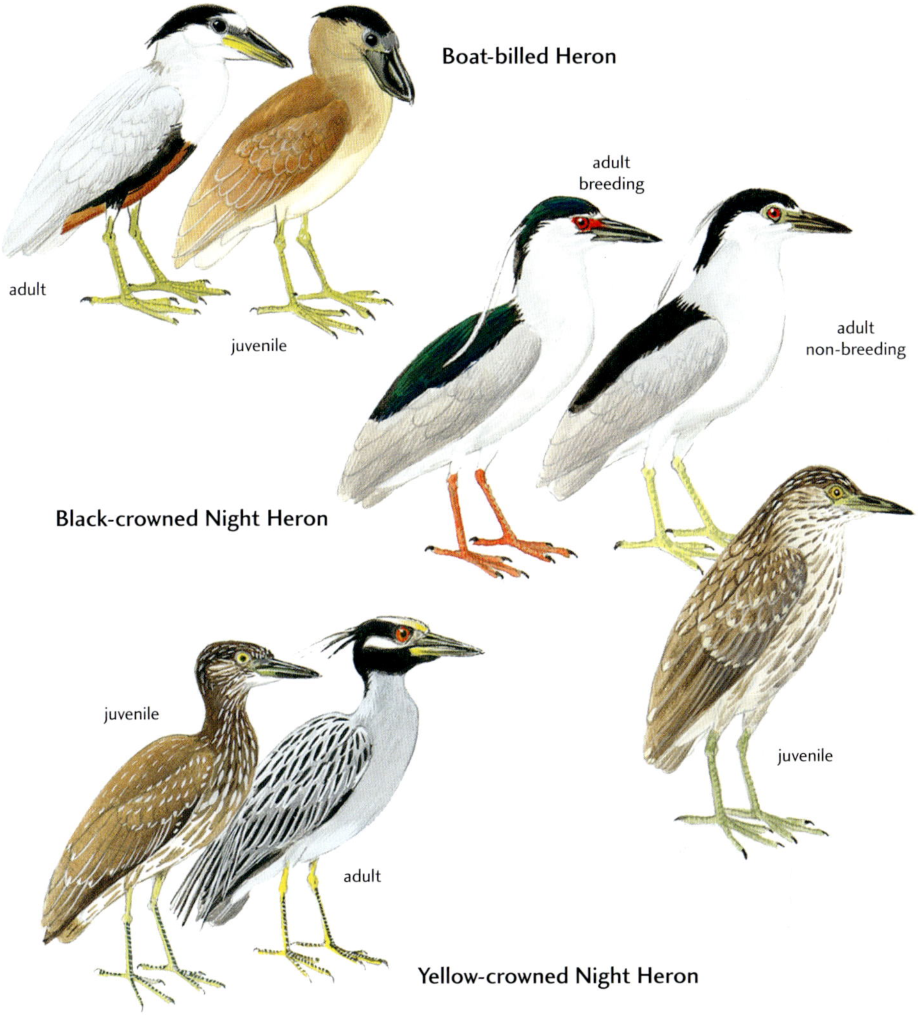
Boat-billed Heron
adult
juvenile
adult
breeding
adult
non-breeding
Black-crowned Night Heron
juvenile
juvenile
adult
Yellow-crowned Night Heron

adult
non-breeding
adult
breeding
juvenile/
immature
Least Grebe
Pied-billed
Grebe
adult
non-breeding
adult
breeding
juvenile/
immature

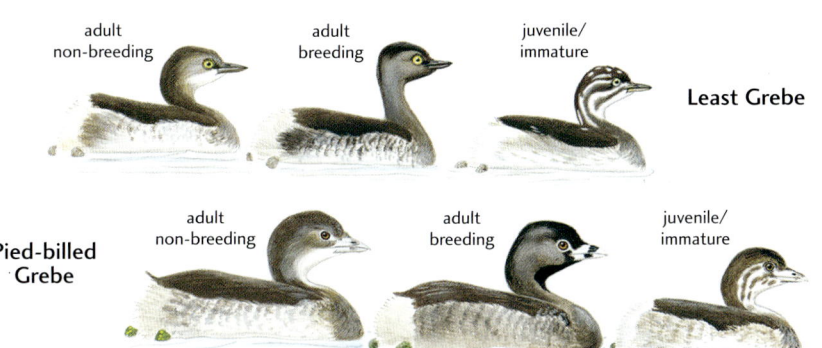

PLATE 15: IBISES

White Ibis *Eudocimus albus* — L 60cm
Ar Ibis blanco; **Bon** Not recorded; **Cur** Ibis blanku; **NL** Witte ibis.
Completely white with black wingtips. Long bill, facial skin and legs red. White iris. Male somewhat larger than female. Immature brown, streaked head and neck and brown wings. Underparts white. Bill and legs brownish. Resembles immature Scarlet Ibis but *paler with no pink hue*. With age they turn whiter and whiter. **Voice** When feeding in groups a low nasal grunt. May give soft honks. **HH** Forages in shallow water, probing mud for worms and molluscs. Mixes readily with other ibises, egrets and herons. **Status** Regular visitor in Bubali pond on Aruba. On Curaçao only observed once. Visitor from South America during the dry season there.

Scarlet Ibis *Eudocimus ruber* — L 58cm
Ar Ibis corá; **Bon**, **Cur** Ibis korá; **NL** Rode ibis.
Unmistakable, with bright red plumage. Bill, facial skin and legs reddish-pink. Bill turns black in breeding season. Immature like immature White Ibis, but will soon develop a *pinkish hue to its feathers*. Gradually changes to pale pink, pink and eventually red. **Voice** Mostly silent but in groups utters low nasal grunts. **HH** Probes mud in shallow water for prey but may also be found on dry land looking for insects. Visits fresh waters as well as mangrove mudflats and shallow inner bays. Mixes readily with other ibises, egrets and herons. **Status** Regular visitor in Bubali pond on Aruba, rare visitor on Bonaire and Curaçao. Visitor from South America.

White-faced Ibis *Plegadis chihi* — L 58cm
Ar Ibis cara blanco; **Bon**, **Cur** Not recorded; **NL** Witmaskeribis.
Like Glossy Ibis but with facial skin and eye red. Legs reddish and shorter than in Glossy Ibis. *Facial skin completely bordered by white feathers* which continue under the bill and extend to around the eye. In non-breeding plumage much duller but distinguishable from Glossy Ibis by more extensive white streaking on head and neck. Immature indistinguishable from immature Glossy Ibis. **Voice** Single birds silent. In groups utters soft guttural contact calls. **HH** Mudflats, shallow freshwater ponds and mangrove flats, where it probes the mud for worms and molluscs. **Status** Rare visitor. One record in the Bubali pond on Aruba, probably exceptional as the normal distribution is from western North America and southern South America.

Glossy Ibis *Plegadis falcinellus* — L 58cm
Ar Ibis preto; **Bon**, **Cur** Ibis pretu; **NL** Zwarte ibis.
Large wading bird with long, downcurved bill. Often looks black, but in good light body plumage is dark bronze, while the wings have a green to purple sheen. Bill and legs greenish-grey. Facial skin grey, in breeding plumage with a white border. Immature paler and duller with streaking on head and neck. Legs longer than tail when seen in flight. **Voice** Single birds mostly silent. In groups gives crooning grunts. **HH** Found by freshwater ponds or the muddy soil underneath mangroves and in salt pans where it probes the mud for worms and molluscs. Also hunts for insects on dry land. **Status** Visitor from South America. Regular visitor in the Bubali pond on Aruba, rare on Bonaire and Curaçao.

PLATE 16: SPOONBILL, STORK, VULTURE AND OSPREY

Roseate Spoonbill *Ajaia ajaja*   L 80cm
Ar Cucharón cora; **Bon**, **Cur** Kucharón kora; **NL** Rode lepelaar.
Tall, superficially stork-like bird. Adult delicate pink with grey bald head, black band at base of neck and unmistakable large *spatulate bill*. Red bars across wings. Eyes and legs red. Immature white with feathered head, yellowish bill, greyish-yellow legs. **Voice** Repeated grunts *huh-huh-huh* and a dry *rrekekekek*. **HH** Frequents inner bays, mangrove growths, tidal pools. Not often seen in fresh waters. Feeds by moving its bill back and forth through the water, filtering out small organisms. **Status** Rare visitor from South America to the islands but reported from all three islands.

Wood Stork *Mycteria americana*   L 100cm, W 160cm
Ar Ciguieña amerikana; **Bon**, **Cur** Not recorded; **NL** Kaalkopooievaar.
Large white wading bird with bare black head and neck. Flight feathers and legs black. Long decurved black bill. Immature similar but more greyish. Head and neck with downy feathers. Bill grey to yellowish. **Voice** Generally silent. In breeding colonies bill-clapping and occasional grunts can be heard. **HH** Bird of fresh water, inner bays and marshes, often in large groups. Will wade through the water with half-opened bill and snap up prey. **Status** Rare visitor from South America. One record of an immature bird staying for months in the Bubali pond on Aruba.

Turkey Vulture *Cathartes aura*   L 66–76cm
Ar Zamuro cabez còrà; **Bon**, **Cur** Not recorded; **NL** Kalkoengier.
Large black bird with long 'fingers' on wingtips in flight. Wings show two clear tones: **underwing-coverts are dark, contrasting with the light brown flight feathers**. Characteristic flight pattern in which the wings are held in a shallow 'V' in a tilting, gliding flight path. **Bare head and neck red** with white patch across nape (*C. a. ruficollis*) or all red (*C. a. meridionalis*). Large, ivory-coloured bill. Two-toned wing pattern also found in Lesser and Greater Yellow-headed Vulture but these clearly show yellow head. *C. a. ruficollis* is resident in northern South America, *C. a. meridionalis* is a migrant from North America. **Voice** Mostly silent. When feeding hissing noises and grunts may be heard. **HH** One of the few birds with a keen sense of smell. Feeds on carcasses. Will soar to look for roadkill or other carrion. Generally will not gather in groups like the Black Vulture and tends to stay closer to the ground. **Status** Rare visitor. One observation on Aruba of a bird flying high overhead. Consequently the ssp. could not be determined.

Osprey *Pandion haliaetus*   L 55–60cm, W 150–170cm
Ar Gabilan piscador; **Bon**, **Cur** Gabilan piskadó; **NL** Visarend.
In flight the **long, angled, 'fingered' wings** are characteristic. Underside is white with a black spot at the wrist. Mainly dark brown above. Head white with black band through the eye. The nuchal crest gives untidy appearance. Tail with narrow brown bands. Immature crown and underparts streaked brown. Local birds belong to *P. h. carolinensis* from North America. **Voice** Utters plaintive high-pitched *whee-whee* calls. **HH** All along the coast but also in freshwater ponds that hold large fish. Cruising at low altitude along the coast, it will dive in shallow waters to grasp fish with its claws, carrying it to some high feeding place to eat it. Not a shy bird, it will venture near human habitation and busy roads. **Status** Regular visitor from North America but present throughout the year.

PLATE 17: KITES, HARRIER AND HAWK

Swallow-tailed Kite *Elanoides forficatus* L 60cm
Ar Milano rab'i swalchi; **Bon** Milano rab'i souchi; **Cur** Not recorded; **NL** Zwaluwstaartwouw.
Incredibly slender, elegant, black-and-white bird. Unmistakable with long pointed wings and *deeply forked, scissor-like tail*. Head, neck, underparts and underwing-coverts white. Back, wings and tail black, though the tertials may show a variable amount of white. Eyes red. Bill and relatively small feet greyish-black. Immature head and breast more buff-coloured and streaked with grey-brown. **Voice** Usually silent but may emit shrill high-pitched whistles when competing for prey. **HH** Almost always in groups. Will swoop through the air chasing insects, especially when leaf-cutting ants swarm with the first rains. Also plucks lizards and small birds out of trees. **Status** Rare visitor from South America (race *yetapa*) or North American (nominate). One record on Aruba and another on Bonaire.

White-tailed Kite *Elanus leucurus* L 38cm
Ar Milano rabo blanco; **Bon**, **Cur** Not recorded; **NL** Amerikaanse grijze wouw.
Only raptor to give an *all-white impression*. Pearly grey above, underparts white. Small black spot around the eye, black spot on the shoulder. Black mark on the underside of the wing at the wrist. Iris red. Yellow legs and cere, black bill. Long tail rather square. Immature streaked brown above and on breast and tail, large black wing patch. Record relates to the South American nominate ssp. **Voice** A short high whistle *kweep* and also a whistle followed by a grunt. **HH** Very elegant falcon-like raptor. Hunts mainly at dawn and dusk, for rodents but will readily take lizards too. Often hunts along tree lines. Will hover. **Status** Rare visitor from South America. One record on Aruba.

Northern Harrier *Circus cyaneus* L 50–60cm
Ar, **Bon** Not recorded; **Cur** Gabilan car'i palabrua; **NL** Blauwe kiekendief.
Slender raptor with owl-like face and a *conspicuous white rump* in both sexes. Sexual dimorphism. Male pale grey with black wingtips, lightly barred below, tail with several narrow darker bands, yellow feet. Facial disc whitish. Female brown, white supercilium, underparts buff streaked heavily with brown. Facial disc more buff. Tail with broader bands than in male. Immature like female but underparts all buff with only breast and throat streaked with brown. **Voice** A sharp *kek-kek-kek* as alarm call. Whistling during aerial display performed in the breeding season. **HH** Tilting flight back and forth low over the ground characteristic, looking for rodents and lizards. **Status** Rare visitor from North America. One record from Curaçao (Klein Hofje) of a subadult bird.

White-tailed Hawk *Geranoaetus albicaudatus* L 55cm, W 120cm
Ar, **Cur** Partawela; **Bon** Gabilan di seru; **NL** Witstaartbuizerd.
Largest raptor on the islands. Light morph slate grey above, head and head-sides also grey giving the bird a hooded appearance. Shoulders rufous. Underside white, *tail white with a dark subterminal band*. Feet yellow. Dark morph slate grey all over but also with white tail. Immature brown with dark grey tail, marked with many narrow dark bars. Light supercilium. Birds from the islands belong to the rather small and pale resident race of *B. a. colonus* which also occurs in northern South America. **Voice** Utters a surprisingly soft whistle *kee-wee*, repeatedly. **HH** In flight the *rounded, broad, somewhat fingered wings* are characteristic. Often hangs still in the air, balancing itself against the breeze. **Status** Breeds on all three islands, though may be close to extinction on Aruba and Bonaire. **Note** Formerly placed in *Buteo*.

PLATE 18: CARACARAS AND FALCONS

Crested Caracara *Caracara cheriway* — L 55–60cm, W 120cm
Ar, **Bon**, **Cur** Warawara; **NL** Kuifcaracara.
In flight recognisable by *heavy bill*. Dark brown wings, back and belly. Breast and hindneck buff barred with brown. Sides of head buff, crown dark brown. Red facial skin and base of bill. Tail buff with numerous dark bars. Feet yellow. Immature lighter brown, streaked with white. Facial skin and base of bill pale pink, feet pale. In flight heavy, rowing wingbeats characteristic. **Voice** A raucous rattle, with the bird throwing its head backwards. Mostly heard in the morning. **HH** Feeds mainly on carrion. Often perches on top of candelabra cacti. Usually seen in pairs but small groups may form. Enters farms to pick up whatever offal it can find. **Status** Breeds on all three islands. Nests are large constructions of twigs and branches, usually in candelabra cacti.

Yellow-headed Caracara *Milvago chimachima* — L 40–45cm
Ar Not recorded; **Bon**, **Cur** Warawara kabes hel; **NL** Geelkopcaracara.
Notably smaller than Northern Crested Caracara. In flight the *long wings, long tail* and a somewhat erratic flight pattern with a rather laborious 'butterfly-stroke' stand out. Upperparts dark brown. Wing-coverts and tertials have whitish tips, giving the wings a spotted appearance. Underwings with conspicuous *large white patches*. Creamy-buff head, neck, breast and belly. Bill and feet whitish. Tail buff with numerous black bands. Immature profusely streaked below. **Voice** A grating descending high scream *scriiiiiiiiii*. **HH** Feeds on carrion but may hunt lizards, nestlings and small rodents. Usually seen in pairs. May follow cattle. **Status** Rare visitor from South America, One record on Curaçao and one on Bonaire.

American Kestrel *Falco sparverius* — L 25cm
Ar, **Bon**, **Cur** Kinikini; **NL** Amerikaanse torenvalk.
Small reddish-brown falcon. *Pointed wings and long tail with dark subterminal band are conspicuous in flight*. Male with grey wings, female with black-barred brown wings. In both sexes grey crown and black 'whiskers' bordering white cheeks characteristic. Male with reddish-brown tail with broad black terminal band and narrow white edge. Tail of female with numerous narrow black bars. The endemic ssp. on Curaçao and Aruba, *F. s. brevipennis*, is characterised by its small size, short wings, reduced barring on the upperparts and creamy tinges on the underparts and dark grey crown in male. **Voice** Utters a penetrating and fast *kee-kee-kee*. **HH** Often seen perched on high observation post from which it will swoop down on its prey – lizards, small birds and insects. May hover. **Status** Breeds on Aruba and Curaçao but is only a visitor to Bonaire.

Merlin *Falco columbarius* — L 25cm
Ar, **Bon**, **Cur** Kinikini grandi; **NL** Smelleken.
Same size as American Kestrel but much sturdier build. In flight *shorter, broader wings and shorter tail distinguish it*. In male upperparts all bluish-grey with white hindneck and sides of neck rufous streaked with black. Female brown above, larger than male. Underparts in both sexes buff streaked with brown. Tail with a broad black terminal band. Immature like female. Tail grey with 3–4 dark bands. Small size and lack of a striking face pattern help identification. Birds visiting the islands belong to the northern North American nominate ssp. **Voice** High-pitched whistles. Alarm call an accelerating *tweetweeweetweetwee*. **HH** Hunts by chasing birds in close pursuit. Determined, fast straight flight quite unlike American Kestrel. May flush small waterfowl by approaching them repeatedly with great speed. **Status** Regular winter visitor from North America but present on Bonaire almost throughout the year.

Peregrine Falcon *Falco peregrinus* — L 40–50cm
Ar, **Bon**, **Cur** Falki peregrino; **NL** Slechtvalk.
Largest falcon on the islands. Female considerably larger and heavier than male. Recognisable by its *strong facial pattern with black 'teardrop' markings*. Upperparts all bluish-grey, white underparts heavily spotted dusky, almost forming cross bars. Immature brown with streaked underparts. Most birds recorded on the islands belong to the ssp. *F. p. tundrius* which is smaller, paler, with less barring and spotting and narrower sideburns than *F. p. anatum*. The latter may be expected to pass by the islands. **Voice** Not often heard. Alarm call a raucous *rehk-rehk-rehk*. Otherwise a repeated *kek*. **HH** Powerful flight from which it may stoop on prey below. Will take waders, doves, egrets and ducks. May flush waterfowl by making repeated passes at flocks. Once caught it will take the prey to a preferred feeding perch. **Status** Winter visitor from North America. May return to same hunting grounds year after year.

PLATE 19: RAIL, GALLINULES AND COOTS

Sora *Porzana carolina*   L 21cm
Ar Gaito sora; **Bon, Cur** Gaitu sora; **NL** Soraral.
Secretive marsh bird. **Cocked tail with white undertail-coverts**. Brown above, mottled with black and white. Face grey with black mask, the black extending in a line running from throat to breast. Underparts barred black and white. Yellow bill and greenish legs. In female black line down throat does not reach breast. Immature lacks black on head, much browner all over, but has yellow bill with black surround. **Voice** Rarely calls out in winter but a plaintive *ker-wee?* may be heard. When disturbed gives a loud *kek*. **HH** Found after heavy rains at the borders of all kinds of freshwater pools and ponds. Creeps through the undergrowth and rarely shows itself. **Status** Regular winter visitor from North America. May stay for months at a time in the same place near permanent freshwater ponds.

Purple Gallinule *Porphyrio martinicus*   L 30cm
Ar Gaito biña; **Bon, Cur** Gaitu biña; **NL** Amerikaans purperhoen.
Beautiful slender marsh bird, violet-blue colour unlike any other bird on the islands. Pale blue frontal shield and bright red bill with yellow tip. Wings have bronze sheen. Undertail-coverts black. Immature wings also have bronze sheen but immature otherwise pale brown. Downy chick black. **Yellow bill with black spot** distinguishes it from chicks of Common Gallinule and Caribbean Coot. **Voice** Has a great variety of calls – cackles, guttural grunts and laughs. Alarm call a sharp *kek-kek-kek*. Also a high-pitched, rattling shriek. **HH** Inhabits fresh water with plenty of vegetation. Keeps more to shore vegetation than Common Gallinule and not often seen swimming. Often seen traipsing over floating water plants. **Status** Visitor from both North and South America. Suspected to breed in very wet years but no reliable data so far. **Note** Formerly placed in *Porphyrula*.

Common Gallinule *Gallinula galeata*   L 35cm
Ar Gaito pico corá; **Bon** Gaitu pik korá; **Cur** Patu pik korá; **NL** Amerikaans waterhoen.
Dark grey to black bird with white line along flanks. Red frontal shield and bill with yellow tip. Long, greenish legs and toes. White undertail-coverts with black centre. Immature brownish-grey, distinguished from immature Purple Gallinule by **white flank line**. Chick black with bare crown and **red, yellow-tipped bill**. Birds on the islands belong to the West Indian ssp. *G. g. cerceris*. The South American nominate ssp. with yellow legs and red tibia may occur as migrant but so far has not been recorded. **Voice** A whirring rattle and harsh *kek-kek-kek* in alarm or as warning to conspecifics. Also shorter *kuk* notes when feeding. **HH** Freshwater bird. Swims in open water more often than Purple Gallinule. Swims with cocked tail, showing white undertail-coverts. Also feeds on land and on shore vegetation. **Status** Has become breeding bird since permanent freshwater ponds have become established on the islands. Breeding recorded on all three islands.

Caribbean Coot *Fulica caribaea*   L 35–40cm
Ar Gaito frente blanco; **Bon** Gaitu frente blanku; **Cur** Patu ckokwèkwè; **NL** Caribische meerkoet.
Dark grey to black, rather plump waterbird with white bill, **large bulbous frontal shield** and white undertail-coverts. Reddish band near tip of bill. Legs greenish-yellow. Immature paler with more white on underparts. Distinguished from American Coot by bulbous, not flat, frontal shield which is white or sometimes yellowish-orange but never chestnut-red. Chick dark grey with orange feathers on head and shoulders, red bare hindcrown and **bill red with white tip**. **Voice** Soft clucks when feeding. Various cackling and croaking sounds can also be heard. A loud rattling *krrrrr-krrrr* when chasing off conspecifics. **HH** Found on all freshwater ponds where it will swim in the open, diving for aquatic vegetation. Mostly in pairs which will defend their space by chasing off intruders. **Status** Has established itself as breeding bird in the permanent freshwater ponds on the islands. Numbers may swell to the hundreds in winter by visitors from other parts of the Caribbean.

American Coot *Fulica americana*   L 35–40cm
Ar Gaito pico blancu; **Bon, Cur** Gaito pik blanku; **NL** Amerikaanse meerkoet.
Similar to Caribbean Coot, but has **smaller and narrower frontal shield, flat with only a small reddish-brown knob near the base**. Legs yellow with red tibiae which can be seen when the bird is swimming away from the observer. However, the colour of the tibiae may vary with age and with the advance of the breeding season. Dark brown band near tip of bill. **Voice** Various cackling and clucking noises. Male and female separable by voice; alarm is sharp *puhlk* in male and a softer *poonk* in female, and male threatening call is *puhk-kuk-kuk*, in female *kaw-prow*. It would be worthwhile to listen for the courting call of males, a coughing *perk-perk-perk*, as this might indicate breeding attempts. **HH** Same habitat and behaviour as Caribbean Coot. Found among large flocks of Caribbean Coot and hence easily overlooked. **Status** Visitor from North America. Formerly considered conspecific with Caribbean Coot, which explains why there are few data on its occurrence on the islands. However, recent data suggest that it is a winter visitor to the islands but in small numbers. Breeding is suspected but no completely reliable data have been gathered.

PLATE 20: LIMPKIN, THICK-KNEE, LAPWING AND PLOVERS

Limpkin *Aramus guarauna* — L 65–70cm
Ar Garao; **Bon**, **Cur** Not recorded; **NL** Koerlan.
Somewhat resembles an ibis but more slender and bill almost straight. Overall chocolate brown with head and neck profusely streaked white, more densely on head. Feathers have lighter edges. Long, slightly drooping bill yellowish with dark tip. Legs and feet long and black. **Voice** Mostly heard between dusk and dawn when it reacts to sudden noise by uttering an unmistakable *ca-rra-oooou*. Otherwise has a large repertoire of unusual noises, compared to a human in distress. **HH** Fresh water, the shores of inner bays, edges of mangroves. Bird of marshy vegetation where it probes the mud for snails and worms. **Status** Rare visitor from South America. Only one record from Aruba where a bird stayed several days.

Southern Lapwing *Vanellus chilensis* — L 35cm
Ar, **Bon**, **Cur** Kivit; **NL** Chileense kievit.
Bold black and white pattern on wings and deep wingbeats characteristic. Buff above with bronze-green sheen. Breast black, belly white. Head and neck grey contrasting with black forehead and black line running down from chin. Conspicuous nuchal crest. Red eyes and legs, yellow bill. Immature brown-grey barred with black on crown and nape, and white wingbars as adult. **Voice** Very noisy. Will utter loud *kee-kee-kee* cry at the least disturbance. **HH** Usually in pairs but may form large groups outside breeding season. Bird of open grassland but can also be found on strips of grass at road sides. **Status** Irregular visitor from South America. Known from five records on Aruba where nest defence behaviour was observed, though no further evidence of breeding. Three records on Bonaire and one on Curaçao.

Double-striped Thick-knee *Burhinus bistriatus* — L 40–45cm
Ar, **Bon** Not recorded; **Cur** Snepi di mondi; **NL** Caribische griel.
Rather large, upright bird. Upperparts brown streaked white, throat and belly white. Remarkably large yellow eyes. White supercilium bordered above by black line. Relatively heavy legs. Belly and under-tail coverts white. In flight shows black wings with white 'windows'. Underwings white. **Voice** Call, given at night, similar to that of Southern Lapwing, *kee-kee-kee*. Also shrill *da-ra da-ra*. **HH** Visits dry open country where it will rest during daytime in the shadows of small bushes, becoming active at dusk. Can run very fast. **Status** Rare visitor from South America, One old record on Curaçao. However, the fact that a local name for it exists suggests that once it may have been more common.

Killdeer *Charadrius vociferus* — L 25cm
Ar Lopi doble coyar; **Bon**, **Cur** Lopi doble koyar; **NL** Killdeerplevier.
Immediately recognisable by its size and the **double breast band**. Brownish above with rufous rump and tail. Tail has black terminal band with a white margin. Red eye-ring. Bill slender, black and legs yellowish-pink. Conspicuous white bars on wings. Immature duller overall. The birds from the islands belong to the ssp. *C. v. ternominatus*, which is smaller and greyer than other ssp. **Voice** Most vociferous of plovers, alarms with loud *kill-dee, kill-dee*. **HH** Found on muddy shores of lagoons, behind mangroves and near temporary pools in the rainy season. Usually in pairs or single birds. **Status** Regular visitor and breeding bird. Breeding reported from Aruba and Curaçao. In winter visitors from North America arrive.

American Golden Plover *Pluvialis dominica* — L 25cm
Ar Lopi dorado; **Bon**, **Cur** Lopi dorá; **NL** Amerikaanse goudplevier.
Resembles Black-bellied Plover but smaller and **more golden-brown**. Upperparts brown speckled with gold, underparts slightly mottled grey. Light supercilium. Breeding plumage also resembles that of Black-bellied Plover but the upperparts are of a golden colour and the black on the underparts runs **all the way to the undertail-coverts**, unlike in the Black-bellied Plover. In rest wingtips extend beyond the tip of the tail. In flight undersides of wings brown, no black 'armpits' and no white rump. Overall gives a much darker impression than Black-bellied Plover. **Voice** A melodious two-syllable whistle *weedletee* often heard when bird passes overhead. **HH** Usually in small groups or singly, though sometimes in large groups of up to 100. Occurs on mudflats of salt pans, shores of freshwater ponds and inner bays or after heavy rains on flooded land. **Status** Regular visitor from North America though less frequent than Black bellied Plover.

Black-bellied Plover *Pluvialis squatarola* — L 30cm
Ar lopi gris; **Bon**, **Cur** Lopi shinishi; **NL** Zilverplevier.
Sturdy wader with round head and large eyes. Gives an all-grey impression but upperparts finely speckled white, underparts white. Light supercilium. In breeding plumage face, cheeks, breast and underparts black up to rump. A white border separates the black from crown, neck and flanks. Black feet and bill. When visible, the very short hind toe is a determining feature. In rest wingtips do not protrude beyond tail-tip. In flight shows conspicuous **black 'armpits', white wingbar, white rump and lightly barred tail**. These features make it easy to distinguish from American Golden Plover. **Voice** Mostly silent but utters a plaintive whistled *pee-o-wee?* when disturbed. **HH** Will dwell wherever there is water. In pairs or small groups, can be found on rocky shores, sandy beaches, salt pans, mangrove edges and freshwater ponds. Feeds on small molluscs and crustaceans. **Status** Regular visitor from North America. Most numerous during winter and springtime passage. [Alt: Grey Plover]

PLATE 21: SMALLER PLOVERS

Piping Plover *Charadrius melodus* — L 17cm
Ar, **Cur** Not recorded; **Bon** Lopi melódiko; **NL** Dwergplevier.
Very pale, sandy-coloured plover. Looks like Snowy Plover but larger, *no black ear patches and has a complete or nearly complete dark breast band*. Bill yellow with black tip, *legs yellow*. In winter breast band grey, bill all black and also legs turn dark. White of forehead does not extend beyond the eye. In flight the white wingbars are conspicuous as are the white uppertail-coverts. **Voice** A piping and quite penetrating *peep, peep-lo*. **HH** Bird of seacoast. Found on sandy beaches and coral rubble. **Status** Rare visitor from North America. Two records from Bonaire.

Semipalmated Plover *Charadrius semipalmatus* — L 17cm
Ar, **Bon**, **Cur** Lopi semipalmata; **NL** Amerikaanse bontbekplevier.
Small shorebird with a relatively large head. Uniformly brown above with white forehead continuing in white eyestripe. White of chin and throat extends to a *white collar all around the neck*, which distinguishes it from Collared Plover. One single brown band across chest, becoming black in summer. Short dark bill with yellow base and yellow legs with webbed toes. In summer yellow on bill more extensive. **Voice** A clear liquid two-syllable whistle *tee-wee* with a rising inflection. **HH** Prefers sea shore and mudflats to forage. Often in mixed groups with other waders. When foraging alternates bouts of running with sudden stops to pick at small prey. Feeds on small molluscs, crustaceans and in salt pans especially salt flies. **Status** Regular winter visitor from North America.

Wilson's Plover *Charadrius wilsonia* — L 19cm
Ar Lopi pico diki; **Bon**, **Cur** Lopipik diki; **NL** Dikbekplevier.
Most conspicuous feature of this plover is its disproportionately *long, heavy, all-black bill*. In non-breeding plumage is yellowish-brown overall. Head-pattern similar to Semipalmated Plover but can be distinguished by its larger size. *Dark-brown chest-band broader than in Semipalmated and turning to rufous patches on sides of chest*. In breeding plumage the overall colour is much darker and more uniform. Bill black, legs pinkish-grey. The residents belong to the ssp *C. w. cinnamominus*, which is more rufous throughout than the migrant North American nominate ssp., which is paler grey and less brown above, with a black breastband in male and uniformly pale-brown in female. **Voice** Soft whistle *weet*. When alarmed a stronger *quit, quit-it*. **HH** Inhabits the mudflats of the salt pans but can also be found on coral walls at the sea shore. **Status** Breeding bird and regular visitor. Breeds on all three islands and is joined by visitors from North America in winter.

Snowy Plover *Charadrius nivosus* — L 15cm
Ar Lopi blanco; **Bon**, **Cur** Lopi blanku; **NL** Strandplevier.
Small, very pale, fast-running shorebird. *Black legs, slender black bill and black ear patch* distinguish it from Piping Plover. Upperparts light coffee-and-cream colour, underparts white. Black forecrown. Black patch at side of chest in male but imm., female and winter male. White of forehead extends beyond the eye. This species was until recently considered conspecific with Kentish Plover *C. alexandrinus*, which replaces Snowy Plover in the Old World. **Voice** Usually silent but when excited utters quite melodious trilling calls, *trrreeee-oo*. **HH** Occurs on mudflats in salt pans and partly dried-out lagoons. Usually in pairs or small groups. Often builds its nest on the dams separating the salt pans. Feeds on salt-flies and their larvae and small crustaceans and snails. **Status** Breeding has been recorded on Bonaire and Curaçao but not on Aruba so far. Less numerous in winter. **Note** Formerly treated as conspecific with Kentish Plover *C. alexandrinus* of the Old World.

Collared Plover *Charadrius collaris* — L 15cm
Ar Lopi coyar; **Bon**, **Cur** Lopi koyar; **NL** Kraagplevier.
Looks like Semipalmated Plover but, in spite of its name, *no white collar going around the neck*. Brown above with lighter patches of cinnamon on head and hindcrown. Forecrown black. White underparts. Black breast band bordered by rufous patches at the sides. Bill black, legs greyish-pink. Immature lacks black and rufous. As a whole makes a more slender, delicate impression than Semipalmated Plover. *Only* **Charadrius** *to lack a nuchal collar*. **Voice** Quiet, but short chirps, *cheep*, *keechup* and a sharp metallic *chip* may be heard. **HH** Prefers sand flats of inner bays or freshwater ponds and temporary pools in the rainy season. Often in mixed flocks with other small plovers. **Status** Regular visitor from South and Central America and possible breeding bird. One record of moulting juveniles on Bonaire is taken as proof of breeding.

PLATE 22: SUNGREBE, JACANA AND PIED SHOREBIRDS

Sungrebe *Heliornis fulica* L 29cm
Ar, **Cur** Not recorded; **Bon** Gaito zambuyadó; **NL** Kleine fuutkoet.
Looks like a cross between a grebe and a coot. Long, grebe-like bill, dull red eye-ring. Male has **conspicuous white and black stripes on sides of neck and also bold black and white pattern on head**. Crown black, white stripe behind eye and black stripe through the eye. Upperparts olive brown, sides buff, foreneck and underparts white. Feet banded black and yellow but seldomly visible. Female similar but with buff cheeks. **Voice** Not often heard. May emit a deep honking, froglike sound *eeoó, eeoó* as warning. **HH** Wary and hence difficult to observe. Will swim deep in the water, sometimes with only the neck visible. When disturbed will take off like a coot, pattering the water and spreading its tail. Freshwater bird. **Status** Rare visitor from South America. One record on Bonaire.

Wattled Jacana *Jacana jacana* L 24cm
Ar, **Bon**, **Cur** Jacana; **NL** Leljacana.
In flight immediately recognisable by its *yellow wings*. Yellow bill and red frontal shield with red wattle very conspicuous. Black head, neck and underparts and wing-coverts chestnut brown. Long pale yellow legs and very long toes. In flight feet extending well beyond the tail. Female larger than male and more brightly coloured. Immature brown above, white below with a long white supercilium. **Voice** When taking flight a loud and indignant *kee-kee-kee*. Chattering noises when feeding. **HH** Inhabits well-vegetated marshy areas but on the islands may be found along the shore. Will walk on floating plants. The female mates with several males, leaving each male to incubate the eggs. **Status** Rare visitor from South America. Two records on Curaçao and one on Bonaire.

Black-necked Stilt *Himantopus mexicanus* L 38cm
Ar Macamba; **Bon** Kaweta di patu; **Cur** Makamba; **NL** Steltkluut.
Strikingly black-and-white shorebird with very long pink legs. Long, pointed black bill. In flight the long legs trailing the tail are conspicuous. Female and immature more brownish on the back. In flight shows black wings with white rump extending to a wedge on lower back. **Voice** Very alert bird which will utter a loud *kek-kek-kek* alarm call by the slightest sign of danger, in this way also alarming other nearby birds. **HH** Usually seen in small noisy groups, readily mixing with Lesser and Greater Yellowlegs. Common in lagoons, salt pans and shallow freshwater ponds on all three islands. Usually nests close to salt or brackish water. In winter may congregate in large groups of hundreds of birds. **Status** Breeding bird. In winter is joined by visitors from North America.

American Avocet *Recurvirostra americana* L 45cm
Ar, **Cur** Not recorded; **Bon** Kaweta di patu bola lantá; **NL** Amerikaanse kluut.
Larger than Black-necked stilt and with a completely white neck. Long, upturned black bill and bluish-grey legs. In summer neck and head take on an exquisite russet colour. In flight white on back runs from tail to neck. Wings show bold black-and-white pattern. **Voice** A two-syllable *kluuiit* with a rising inflection, rather similar to American Oystercatcher but more drawn out. In alarm a monosyllabic *kleet*. **HH** Bird of shallow water. Feeds by sweeping the bill from side to side through the water and vegetable matter sifting out small organisms. **Status** Rare visitor from North America. One record of two birds on Bonaire.

American Oystercatcher *Haematopus palliatus* L 48cm
Ar, **Bon** Kibra kokolishi; **Cur** Shon Piet; **NL** Amerikaanse bonte scholekster.
Unmistakable boldly black-and-white patterned bird with a long red bill. Yellow eyes with orange eye-ring, and pale pink legs. Belly white. In flight broad white tail band and white stripe across wings. Immature browner. Typical quick wingbeats and all-black head and breast separate it from Black Skimmer. Island birds belong to nominate ssp. from North and South America. *H. p. prattii* from offshore islands of Venezuela and Trinidad and Tobago has a considerably longer bill. **Voice** Can be very noisy, emitting a penetrating *peet-peet-peet* whistle. **HH** Wanders on rocky shores and coral walls looking for molluscs and crustaceans in tidal pools and crevices. Mostly seen in pairs which tend to stay in the same area. **Status** Breeding bird. Occurs on all three islands but is rather uncommon. Nests have been found on sandy beaches and on the dams between salt pans.

PLATE 23: LARGE AND MEDIUM-SIZED SANDPIPERS

Greater Yellowlegs *Tringa melanoleuca*   L 35cm
Ar Snepi pia hel grandi; **Bon**, **Cur** Snepi pia hel largu; **NL** Gote geelpootruiter.
Mainly grey, relatively large bird. Wings patterned with white spots, neck and breast streaked brownish. Long yellow legs with rather thick joints. Main differences from Lesser Yellowlegs are *size and the long bill (longer than length of head) which is slightly upturned and two-toned: more grey near the base and more black near the tip*. In flight wings and tail distinctly barred and white rump stands out. In breeding plumage colours are darker, showing more contrast with the white. **Voice** Quite vociferous with a descending flute-like *tu-tu-tu*. **HH** Prefers salt pans but can also be found in fresh water and the shores of inner bays. May bob head repeatedly before taking off when disturbed. **Status** Regular visitor. Present throughout the year but most numerous in winter and spring during migration from and to North America. Less numerous than Lesser Yellowlegs.

Lesser Yellowlegs *Tringa flavipes*   L 26cm
Ar Snepi pia hel chikito; **Bon**, **Cur** Snepi pia hel chikitu; **NL** Kleine geelpootruiter.
Smaller than Greater Yellowlegs. *Bill straight and about the same length as the head*. Long yellow legs but joints not as thick as in Greater Yellowlegs. In flight wings more uniformly dark. Shows white rump and barred tail. In breeding plumage the colours are darker, showing more contrast with white spots. **Voice** Quite penetrating two-toned whistle *tuu-tuu* alarms all other birds in the surroundings. **HH** Occurs on muddy shores of lagoons, salt pans, freshwater ponds, inner bays. Usually in small groups but in winter large flocks of hundreds of birds may form. **Status** Regular visitor. Most numerous during winter migration from North America but present throughout the year.

Solitary Sandpiper *Tringa solitaria*   L 21cm
Ar, **Bon**, **Cur** Snepi solitario; **NL** Amerikaanse bosruiter.
Somewhat Smaller than Lesser Yellowlegs, with dusky green legs. Overall darker above with a *conspicuous white eye-ring*. Slender black bill. Back dark with white spots. In flight tail is *dark with a comb-like dark pattern, dark rump*. The ssp. *T. s. cinnamomea* is somewhat larger and paler than nominate, with dark lores and a pale supraloral spot. **Voice** When disturbed utters a loud *peet-weet-weet*. **HH** Almost always alone along edges of freshwater ponds or behind the mangroves. Bobs head like yellowlegs when foraging. Flight quite erratic. **Status** Regular visitor from North America.

Spotted Sandpiper *Actitis macularia*   L 19cm
Ar, **Bon**, **Cur** Snepi barika pintá; **NL** Amerikaanse oeverloper.
Most readily told by teetering up-and-down gait, as if looking to find its balance. In winter upperparts are greyish-brown with narrow black bars, underparts white. Bill dirty yellow with black tip, legs yellowish and white eyeline. *White 'spur' in front of wing bend* is typical. In flight shows a white wingbar. In summer plumage heavily spotted on throat, breast and flanks. **Voice** Call a disyllabic *pee-wee*, similar to that of Solitary Sandpiper but not as penetrating. **HH** Mudflats at freshwater ponds, salt pans and behind mangroves. Mostly solitary. When flushed it will fly low over the water, make a half-circle and return to shore to watch the intruder while constantly bobbing up and down. **Status** Regular visitor from North America. Common on all three islands but never numerous.

Willet *Catoptrophorus semipalmatus*   L 35–40cm
Ar, **Bon**, **Cur** Snepi ala di strepi; **NL** Willet.
Looks like a very large yellowlegs but has a *heavier blackish bill and bluish-grey legs*. In winter upperparts mainly grey without any spots, underparts white. In summer plumage head, neck, breast and flanks spotted black. White eyeline. In flight easy to distinguish by its *bold black and white wing* pattern. Flies with quivering wing beats. Both *C. s. inornatus* (as described) from Canada and NW America and the smaller and darker nominate from E. North America have been recorded. **Voice** Three-syllable whistle *kee-kee-kee* louder and coarser than Greater Yellowlegs. **HH** Inhabits lagoons, salt pans and the mudflats behind mangroves and on edges of freshwater ponds. Feeds singly or in mixed groups. Also active at night. On the islands seems to feed mainly on small snails. **Status** Irregular visitor from North America but never very numerous. No records from Aruba so far.

PLATE 24: MISCELLANEOUS SHOREBIRDS

Whimbrel *Numenius phaeopus*   L 43cm
Ar Lopi piku doblá; **Bon**, **Cur** Lopi pik doblá; **NL** Regenwulp.
Large, heavy shorebird with a *long decurved bill*. Gives the impression of being lower to the ground than more slender sandpipers but in flight feet extend beyond tail. Upperparts brown with lighter feather edges. Crown with two black stripes and stripe through the eye. Legs greyish. Primary-coverts black, forming a clearly visible patch in flight. Bill black with the lower mandible red at base. Female larger than male. **Voice** Utters a series of rapid, trembling high notes *ti-ti-ti-ti-ti*. On wintering grounds usually silent. **HH** Occurs on mudflats of salt pans and lagoons, but also along sand beaches and on reef walls. **Status** Regular visitor from North America. Seen throughout the year but never in great numbers.

Hudsonian Godwit *Limosa haemastica*   L 35–40cm
Ar Lopi còrá; **Bon**, **Cur** Lopi kòrá; **NL** Rode grutto.
Large wader with a long, slightly upturned bill. In winter plumage mainly grey. *White rump and tail-base, bordered by a broad black band*. Bill pinkish at base, dark at tip. Legs blue-grey. In summer plumage upperparts dark brown with breast and underparts reddish-brown. In flight shows blackish wings with white wingbar, white rump and black tail. **Voice** Mainly silent on wintering grounds but may utter clear whistle *whee-wit* especially in flight. **HH** Mixes with other waders near freshwater ponds. Stays in shallow waters. **Status** Rare visitor from North America. Known from three records on Aruba, five on Bonaire and three on Curaçao.

Upland Sandpiper *Bartramia longicauda*   L 30cm
Ar, **Bon**, **Cur** Snepi Bartram; **NL** Bartrams ruiter.
Long-legged slender bird with *long neck, pigeon-like head and large eyes*. Upperparts, head, neck and breast brown mottled with buff. Belly white. Relatively long, wedge-shaped tail. Strikingly short yellow bill with black tip. Long yellow legs. In flight two-toned upper wings are noticeable with primaries darker than inner wings. Black rump. **Voice** Alarm call a fast *kip-ip-ip-ip*. In flight a whistled *huu-hui*. **HH** Found alone or in small groups along shores of freshwater ponds and salt pans. Feeds among shore vegetation. When landing holds up wings for a moment. **Status** Rare visitor from North America. Two records from Aruba, two from Bonaire and two from Curaçao. Presence seems to depend on the existence of freshwater ponds after heavy rains.

Ruddy Turnstone *Arenaria interpes*   L 22cm
Ar Totolica di awa; **Bon**, **Cur** Totolika di awa; **NL** Steenloper.
Compact, rather short-legged small shorebird. *Pied plumage* makes it immediately recognisable. In winter greyish-brown, in summer much more reddish-brown with a strong black-and white face and breast pattern. On the islands birds show often intermediate plumage, adding to pied appearance. Short black bill strong and slightly upturned. Legs bright orange. In flight shows black and white pattern, with rump, lower back and base of wings white, a white wingbar on dark wings, and dark sides of back and head. Visiting birds belong to ssp. *A. i. morinella* from N Canada and NE Alaska. **Voice** Alarm call, also uttered during flight, a staccato *kuk-kuk-kuk*. **HH** Occurs on rocky coasts and reef walls where it forages between the stones. Also on beaches with rocks where it will look for food between the stones. Very confiding. **Status** Regular visitor from North America. Common throughout the year.

Red Knot *Calidris canutus*   L 26cm
Ar Snepi còrá; **Bon**, **Cur** Snepi kòrá; **NL** Kanoet.
Robust wader, distinguishable from many other grey waders mainly by its size. In winter plumage upperparts uniformly grey with scaled appearance of upperwing-coverts. Underparts white. In flight *rump is slightly paler than tail and back*. In summer plumage underparts are cinnamon and upperparts mottled grey-buff. In springtime intermediate plumage can be encountered. First-year birds more cinnamon than adult non-breeding birds. Visiting birds belong to ssp. *C. c. rufia* from arctic Canada. **Voice** Utters a sharp single note *kit* and a softer but still rather sharp *tweek-tweek*. Both calls given in flight and when feeding. **HH** Found along the shores of salt pans, in particular the former Pekelmeer on Bonaire. Almost always in groups. **Status** Regular visitor from North America, mainly on Bonaire. Not many records from Aruba and Curaçao.

PLATE 25: SMALLER SANDPIPERS

Western Sandpiper *Calidris mauri* — L 16cm
Ar, **Bon**, **Cur** Snepi mauri; **NL** Alaskastrandloper.
Closely resembles Semipalmated Sandpiper. The only difference is **the bill which is somewhat longer and slightly drooping at the tip**. However, short-billed male Westerns and long-billed female Semipalmateds are virtually indistinguishable unless seen next to each other. Legs are longer than in Semipalmated. Summer plumage contains more brown than that of Semipalmated. **Voice** Call is longer, higher and sharper than that of Semipalmated, a high *kree-eet*. **HH** Inhabits same habitat but will wade into somewhat deeper water than the latter species. Will submerge its head more often than Semipalmated. **Status** Regular visitor from North America. Not as numerous as Semipalmated or Least Sandpiper but low number of observations may also be due to difficulty of distinguishing between the species.

Semipalmated Sandpiper *Calidris pusilla* — L 15cm
Ar Snepi gris; **Bon**, **Cur** Snepi pia pretu; **NL** Grijze strandloper.
One of a group of small, brownish-grey sandpipers which are difficult to distinguish from each other. In winter the bird is more greyish and in summer more brownish. On the islands all type of variations between the two may be observed. Belly always white. Short black bill with a thick base. **Feet black** which distinguishes it from Least Sandpiper. Bill straight and shorter than in Western Sandpiper. **Voice** Call a soft, chattery *chirrup* when feeding or when resting in groups. In flight a shriller *chirrr*. **HH** Feeds in shallow water of lagoons, inner bays, salt pans by probing the mud. More likely to forage in the water than Least Sandpiper. May occur in groups of several hundreds. **Status** Regular visitor from North America. Present throughout the year with highest numbers in winter. Most numerous of the small sandpipers except on Bonaire where Western Sandpiper is most common.

Least Sandpiper *Calidris minutilla* — L 14cm
Ar Snepi chikito; **Bon**, **Cur** Snepi chikí; **NL** Kleinste strandloper.
Smaller than previous two species but not by much. Distinguished by **greenish-yellow legs**. Bill thinner at the tip than in Semipalmated and shorter than in Western. Upperparts darker brown and chest more streaked. Shorter legs than Western and more slender than Semipalmated. **Voice** Call a shrill, drawn-out trilled *kreeeet*. **HH** Seen throughout the year on muddy shores of inner bays and freshwater ponds where it forages for small insects. Often in mixed flocks with Semipalmated and Western Sandpipers, allowing for side-by-side comparison. **Status** Regular visitor from North America. Present throughout the year with highest numbers in winter

White-rumped Sandpiper *Calidris fuscicollis* — L 19cm
Ar Snepi patrás blanco; **Bon**, **Cur** Snepi patrás blanku; **NL** Bonaparte's strandloper.
Most easily recognised in flight when it shows the **white uppertail-coverts** for which it is named (wrongly, as it is not the rump which is white). Greyish in winter plumage and more brownish in the summer. Below with many fine spots and streaks, especially on breast. In rest the wing points extend beyond the tail. **Flanks marked with short streaks**. Bill black and thin, feet black. **Voice** Call a very high, metallic screech *pee-eet*. **HH** Seems to prefer the shores of freshwater ponds but can also be found in salt pans and inner bays. Often solitary or in small groups. Often seen when other 'peeps' have already left for their breeding grounds in spring. **Status** Regular visitor from North America.

Baird's Sandpiper *Calidris bairdii* — L 18–19cm
Ar, **Bon**, **Cur** Nepi Baird; **NL** Baird's strandloper.
Very much like White-rumped Sandpiper but **rump dark, not white, though it has white lateral edges**. Upperparts more buff with scaled appearance of upper flight feathers. Breast buff streaked with dark brown, sharply separated from white belly and **no streaking on flanks**. Bill black and legs brownish. Immature darker with head and breast more brownish. White-rumped and Baird's Sandpipers are the only sandpipers with wings extending beyond the tail when they are resting. **Voice** Calls a sharp *chik* and a low trilling *preeeet*. **HH** Found on the shores of freshwater ponds, inner bays and salt pans where it feeds on salt flies. **Status** Rare visitor from North America. One record from Curaçao, one from Aruba and four from Bonaire.

Pectoral Sandpiper *Calidris melanotos* — L 20–23cm
Ar Snepi pecho strepiá; **Bon**, **Cur** Snepi pechu strepiá; **NL** Gestreepte strandloper.
Larger and longer-necked than its allies. **Sharp demarcation between darkly streaked breast and white underparts**. Upperparts brown streaked with black but with snipe-like lighter stripes. Light supercilium and throat. Bill lighter at base, legs greenish-yellow. **Voice** Mostly silent. Call quite snipe-like, a rather hoarse *krriik* or *kr'kr'kr*. **HH** Occurs along freshwater ponds and muddy shores but tends to stay more between the vegetation. When disturbed it behaves like a snipe, flying in zigzags. Usually single or in small groups. **Status** Regular visitor from North America. Not very numerous but present every year especially during the autumn migration.

PLATE 26: SANDPIPERS AND DOWITCHERS

Sanderling *Calidris alba*   L 20cm
Ar Snepi blanco. **Bon**, **Cur** Snepi blanku. **NL** Drieteenstrandloper.
Stands out from other small 'peeps' by size and very pale plumage. Upperparts in non-breeding plumage uniformly **very light grey**. Strong, rather blunt, black bill and greyish-green legs. Prominent **black shoulder spot**. Summer plumage mottled brown all over with white belly. In flight shows white wingbar. Immature darker than non-breeding adult, showing some black feathers in wing and on back. Visiting birds belong to *C. a. rubida* from arctic North America. **Voice** When disturbed a soft *twick*. Also gives a soft but sharp *kreet-weet*. **HH** Visits sand beaches where it runs back and forth with the waves. Also near the water edge of salt pans, especially near the white foam that forms there, to pick up salt flies. Mixes readily with other shorebirds especially Ruddy Turnstones and plovers. **Status** Regular visitor. Found throughout the year but never very numerous.

Dunlin *Calidris alpina*   L 20cm
Ar Not recorded. **Bon**, **Cur** Snepi shinishi. **NL** Bonte strandloper.
May be confused with Sanderling but in winter plumage is **darker grey, especially on the breast, and has a long black bill, drooping at the tip**. In rest typical hunched appearance makes it look almost 'neckless'. Throat white, legs black. In flight shows dark central tail feathers bordered by white sides, and dark rump, narrow white wingbar. Summer plumage unmistakable with large black patch on belly and reddish-brown upperparts. **Voice** Call a drawn-out very thin *kreee*. **HH** Found on muddy shores of freshwater ponds and salt pans. Forages by probing mud. **Status** Rare visitor from North America. Only one record from Curaçao and four from Bonaire.

Stilt Sandpiper *Calidris himantopus*   L 22cm
Ar Snepi pia largo. **Bon**, **Cur** Snepi pia largu. **NL** Steltstrandloper.
Smaller than Lesser Yellowlegs, with which it might be confused, but overall gives a greyer impression, and has **greenish legs**. Upperparts plain grey, white underparts. Long, slightly droopy black bill. **White rump conspicuous in flight**. In summer plumage much browner with heavily barred underparts. White supercilium. **Voice** Mostly silent but may give a plaintive *kiuu* or a soft trill *kiirrrr* in flight. When resting in groups a soft chattering can be heard. **HH** Visits salt pans, shallow waters protected by mangroves and freshwater ponds. Wades in deeper water in a very upright posture. Feeds by 'stabbing' the water in quick repetitions. Seems to eat large numbers of salt flies. **Status** Regular visitor from North America. Present throughout the year.

Buff-breasted Sandpiper *Tryngites subruficollis*   L 20cm
Ar Snepi blònt pico chikito. **Bon**, **Cur** Snepi blònt pik chikí. **NL** Blonde ruiter.
Resembles Upland Sandpiper in upright posture, long neck and round head but is smaller with different tail shape and colour. Main distinguishing feature is its **completely buff-coloured body**, from chin to undertail. Upperparts are dusky with a scaled appearance. Short black bill and yellow legs. Immature darker above with black scapulars and more spots on head and neck. **Voice** A short and low-pitched *tiw* and a trilled *prreeet*. Mostly silent. **HH** Shores of freshwater ponds. When disturbed flies up with wild, erratic wingbeats. **Status** Rare visitor from North America. One record from Bonaire where it was seen on the limestone plateau near the sea, two records from Curaçao at the shores of freshwater ponds in very wet years, and two records from Aruba.

Long-billed Dowitcher *Limnodromus scolopaceus*   L 28cm
Ar, **Bon**, **Cur** Snepi gris grandi. **NL** Grote grijze snip.
Bill only fractionally longer than that of Short-billed Dowitcher, 6–7.5cm compared to 4.5–6cm. There is overlap between shorter-billed males of this species and longer-billed female Short-billeds. Winter plumage much like Short-billed. The dark bars on the tail may be wider. In summer plumage also rusty brown but sides of breast and flanks **streaked, not spotted**. Breast less heavily streaked. **Voice** Different from that of Short-billed: a high, unmelodious, thin *keek*, sometimes repeated in quick succession. **HH** Found on shores of saline lagoons and freshwater ponds. In its summer habitat notably more of a freshwater bird than Short-billed but on the islands both species use same habitat. **Status** Rare visitor from North America. Seven verifiable observations from the islands are known, most of them on Bonaire, but likely to be overlooked due to its similarity to Short-billed Dowitcher.

Short-billed Dowitcher *Limnodromus griseus*   L 28cm
Ar Snepi gris chikito; **Bon**, **Cur** Snepi gris chikí; **NL** Kleine grijze snip.
Snipe-like bird, in winter plumage practically indistinguishable from Long-billed Dowitcher. Both recognisable by the very long black bill. Uniformly grey above and on neck and breast. White line above eye and black line running through the eye. Belly white. In flight shows a wedge-formed white patch on rump and back. Upper tail feathers with narrow dark bands. In summer plumage rusty brown with **dark spots** on sides of breast. Visiting birds belong to the nominate Caribbean ssp., the greyest ssp. **Voice** Best distinguishing feature is its call: a rather melodious *tu-tu-tu* uttered in flight. **HH** Visits shores of saline lagoons and freshwater ponds. Probes the mud with its long bill in quick successive thrusts. **Status** Regular visitor from North America. Seen throughout the year but never in large numbers.

PLATE 27: SNIPE, PHALAROPES AND SKUA

Wilson's Snipe *Gallinago delicata* — L 28cm
Ar, **Bon**, **Cur** Snepi di awa; **NL** Watersnip.
Regular visitor. Most often seen when flushed. Normally sits tight in a hunched position among vegetation and is then very difficult to spot. Brown all over with **extremely long, straight bill. Large eye and striped head stand out**. Light stripes on the wing, underparts white. When flushed it flies in a typical zig-zag pattern, uttering harsh protesting notes. Rufous tail with two black bars and white margin conspicuous. **Voice** In flight a winnowing *whowhowho*. When flushed a raucous *ratch, ratch*. **HH** Along shores of freshwater ponds or freshly flooded flats but always hiding among the vegetation. Probes for food in soft mud or picks up insect larvae in shallow water. **Status** Regular visitor from North America. Abundant in wet years but single birds or small groups can be seen during most of the year.

Wilson's Phalarope *Phalaropus tricolor* — L 23cm
Ar Not recorded; **Bon**, **Cur** Snepi seha grandi; **NL** Grote franjepoot.
Phalaropes are unusual in that females in breeding plumage are more colourful than males. The round head, S-shaped neck and very thin needle-like bill are characteristic. In winter plumage uniformly grey above with white cheeks, throat, breast and underparts. Resembles Lesser Yellowlegs and Stilt Sandpiper but smaller and more uniformly grey with immaculate white head and underparts. In flight shows **no wingbars and a white rump**. In summer plumage female has a black face and a cinnamon neck stripe which blends into stripes on the upper wings. Male duller. **Voice** Not often heard but may emit a small grunt in flight. **HH** To be found on freshwater ponds and saline lagoons. When feeding often spins around, taking quick pecks at the disturbed water for small prey. **Status** Rare visitor from North America. Known from five records on Bonaire and one on Curaçao.

Red Phalarope *Phalaropus fulicarius* — L 22cm
Ar, **Cur** Not recorded; **Bon** Snepi seha pik diki; **NL** Rosse franjepoot.
In winter plumage grey above, white below. Dark patch through the eye. In flight shows white wingbars but **no white on back** in contrast to Northern Phalarope. Overall somewhat paler than the latter species. In summer plumage the female has reddish-brown underparts and a white face bordered by black. Male duller. **Voice** Mostly silent but call much shriller than that from other two species, a high *twiit*. **HH** Much more a bird of the open sea than the other two species, especially in plankton-rich waters. At sea it will swim buoyantly, but when driven ashore by bad weather for example, it can be found in saline lagoons and freshwater ponds. **Status** Rare visitor from North America. Only one record from Bonaire. [Alt: Grey Phalarope]

Red-necked Phalarope *Phalaropus lobatus* — L 19cm
Ar Not recorded; **Bon**, **Cur** Snepi seha pik fini; **NL** Grauwe franjepoot.
Smallest of the phalaropes. In winter grey above, white below and with a black line through the eye. Black, very thin bill and legs dark grey. In flight shows **white wingbars**, in contrast to Wilson's Phalarope, and **white lines on the back**. In summer plumage female has black head with white chin and a rufous neck. Male duller. **Voice** Usually silent but in flight may utter a short *twick*. **HH** May be found at sea but also in saline lagoons and freshwater ponds. Always spins anti-clockwise when feeding. **Status** Rare visitor form North America. Two records from Bonaire and one from Curaçao. [Alt: Northern Phalarope]

Great Skua *Stercorarius skua* — L 53–60cm
Ar, **Bon**, **Cur** Saltadó grandi; **NL** Grote jager.
Uniformly dark brown with conspicuous white patches on the flight feathers. In flight looks very falcon-like. Tail is **wedge-shaped**, bill strong and hooked. South Polar Skua (*S. maccormicki*) may have light head and neck. Immature is either dark brown with light brown tips to all wing-coverts and white patches on flight feathers, or uniformly dark brown with only a small white area at base of primaries. **Voice** Generally silent. **HH** Breeds in the north Atlantic but roams the seas outside the breeding season. **Status** Rare visitor. Only one record at sea between Bonaire and Curaçao but more records from farther out at sea. Observed from the coast in Venezuela.

PLATE 28: JAEGERS

Long-tailed Jaeger *Stercorarius longicaudus* — L 55cm
Ar Saltadó rabo largo; **Bon**, **Cur** Saltadó rabu largu; **NL** Kleinste jager.
In breeding plumage immediately recognisable by very long, pointed central tail feathers which protrude up to 20cm beyond the end of the tail. Outside the breeding season these feathers extend much less. **Adult completely white below, without dark breast band** of Pomarine Jaeger though first-year birds do show a broad breast-band. White collar separates black cap from grey upperparts. Overall more slender and graceful than other Jaegers. Immature shows less of a white flash in wings than immature Parasitic Jaeger. **Voice** Generally silent. **HH** Pelagic in habits. Forms loose flocks. Seems to be less parasitic than the other species. **Status** Rare visitor from North America. One record from Aruba. [Alt: Long-tailed Skua]

Parasitic Jaeger *Stercorarius parasiticus* — L 45cm
Ar, **Bon**, **Cur** Saltadó chikí; **NL** Kleine jager.
Very much like Pomarine Jaeger but *smaller. Elongated tail feathers shorter, pointed at tips and not twisted.* Also shows white patches on flight feathers. Has light and dark phase as in Pomarine, and immature very similar to immature Pomarine. Overall it gives a more slender, falcon-like impression than Pomarine, with more rapid and shallower wingbeats. Also more aggressive in chasing after terns and gulls. Immature has more white in wings than immature of Long-tailed Jaeger. **Voice** Generally silent. **HH** Likeliest jaeger to be seen from shore as it often visits bays frequented by terns and gulls. **Status** Irregular visitor from North America. Various records from sea but also a number of sightings from the coast of jaegers harassing terns, gulls and boobies. [Alt: Arctic Skua]

Pomarine Jaeger *Stercorarius pomarinus* — L 55cm
Ar, **Bon**, **Cur** Saltadó mediano; **NL** Middelste jager.
Adult jaegers have elongated central tail feathers, which in Pomarine are *twisted along their shafts and broad at tips, forming 'spoons'*. Dark morph is dark brown all over with white patches on the flight feathers. Light morph is white below with white chin and white collar around the neck and a narrow brown breast band. Strong, hooked bill, yellow with dark tip. Immature lacks the protruding tail feathers and has heavily barred pale rump and underparts. **Voice** Generally silent. **HH** Usually solitary but may form flocks when migrating. Chases after terns and gulls to rob them of their prey. **Status** Irregular visitor from North America. Various records from sea but also seen once above the Bubali pond on Aruba. [Alt: Pomarine Skua]

Long-tailed Jaeger

juvenile pale morph
juvenile intermediate morph
juvenile dark morph
juvenile very dark morph
first-winter/first-summer
second-summer/second-winter
adult summer
adult winter

Parasitic Jaeger

juvenile intermediate morph
third-summer/third-winter
adult summer
adult winter
juvenile pale intermediate morph
first-winter/first-summer

Pomarine Jaeger

adult summer pale morph
adult winter pale morph
juvenile pale morph
juvenile intermediate morph
juvenile dark morph
second-summer/second-winter

PLATE 29: GULLS I

Black-headed Gull *Chroicocephalus ridibundus* — L 37cm
Ar, **Cur** Not recorded; **Bon** Kahela Oropeo; **NL** Kokmeeuw.
Resembles Bonaparte's Gull but slightly larger and *hood more brown than black*. *Red legs and bill*. In flight the underwings show quite *a lot of black*. White leading edge to wings widens and extends into the black tips of the primaries. In winter plumage head white with black ear patch. Bill stays red though. Immature like winter plumage but with dark tail band, shows same underwing pattern of ad., bill ochre at base. **Voice** Harsh, high-pitched cries *kraaah* or a more drawn-out *krreeer*. **HH** Coastal bird, found in harbours and inner bays but not inland. **Status** Rare visitor from North America. One record from the coast of Bonaire.

Bonaparte's Gull *Chroicocephalus philadelphia* — L 33cm
Ar Not recorded; **Bon**, **Cur** Kahela Bonaparte; **NL** Kleine kokmeeuw.
Small gull with upperparts light grey and *white triangular patch at wingtips*. Underwings a two-toned grey but *no black*. In summer plumage has black hood, red legs and *black bill*. Black hood does not extend as far down as in Laughing Gull. In winter white head with a black ear patch. Immature like winter plumage but with narrow black tail band. **Voice** High nasal *cheerp*, when feeding a shorter *chirp*. **HH** Coastal bird, may visit inner bays and freshwater ponds. Flight pattern looks tern-like. When surface-feeding dangling legs may touch the water. **Status** Rare visitor from North America. Observed once in Bonaire harbour and twice on Lake Muizenberg on Curaçao.

Franklin's Gull *Leucophaeus pipixcan* — L 40cm
Ar Meuwchi Franklin; **Bon**, **Cur** Not recorded; **NL** Franklin's meeuw.
Resembles smaller Laughing Gull; mantle a lighter grey. In summer plumage a tinge of pink on the chest. Black hood does not extend as far down as in Laughing Gull. Red bill. *In flight shows black wingtips bordered by white and a white band separating them from the grey upperwings*. In winter plumage has more brown on head than Laughing Gull, forming a half hood. Bill black. Immature like second-winter Laughing Gull but more slender with darker hood. **Voice** A shrill *ku-ku-ku* and a more nasal *karr, karr*. Less clear than in Laughing Gull. **HH** More pelagic than Laughing Gull. Tern-like flight, may touch the water with dangling legs. **Status** Rare visitor from North America. Observed twice on Aruba.

PLATE 30: GULLS II

Ring-billed Gull *Larus delawarensis*   L 48cm
Ar Meuwchi pico renchi; **Bon** Kahela pik renchi; **Cur** Not recorded; **NL** Ringsnavelmeeuw.
Resembles Herring Gull but smaller and slighter. *Bill yellow with a black ring near the tip. Black wingtips have only two white spots. Legs yellowish-green.* Iris yellow. Immature difficult to distinguish from immature Herring Gull; somewhat paler and black tail band tends to be more sharply defined against more immaculate white tail feathers, also spotted rather than mottled brown. Immature iris dark, bill pinkish with black tip. Full breeding plumage reached after two years. **Voice** Shrill mewing *ki-eeuw*, higher than in Herring Gull. **HH** Found along the coast. Tends to mix with other gulls. **Status** Rare visitor from North America. Two records on Aruba and three from Bonaire, all first- or second-winter birds.

Laughing Gull *Leucophaeus atricilla*   L 42cm
Ar Meuwchi haridó; **Bon**, **Cur** Kahela komun; **NL** Lachmeeuw.
Its loud cackling laugh makes this gull quite easy to recognise. In summer plumage the *black head with white 'eyelids' and red bill and legs* are distinctive. Upperparts are dark grey with black wingtips. *In flight shows a white trailing edge to the wing.* Grey of upper wing blends into black wingtips, *no white in wingtips*. In winter plumage the head is white with the back of the crown mottled brown extending to the eye. Bill and feet are black. Immature dark greyish-brown, including the whole head, with white rump and tail, ending in a broad brown sub-terminal band. Bill and feet blackish. In second winter head as in adult winter plumage. Birds on the islands belong to the West Indies nominate ssp., smaller than other ssps. **Voice** Clear, high-pitched *ka-ka-ka-ka*, like laughter. **HH** Coastal bird. Often found on the coral rubble at the coast but very seldom in fresh water. **Status** Breeding established with certainty only on Bonaire and on the reef islands of Aruba and possibly on Klein Curaçao. Most numerous between February and September.

Herring Gull *Larus argentatus*   L 60cm
Ar Meuwchi gris; **Bon** Kahela gris; **Cur** Not recorded; **NL** Zilvermeeuw.
Large white gull with pearly grey back and wings. *Strong yellow bill with red spot at the tip. Feet flesh-coloured. Wing tips lack white spots.* Iris pale yellow. Juv. mottled dark brown all over with dark brown bill, each year turning a bit lighter to reach adult plumage in four years. Last traces of immature plumage are brown feathers among grey wing feathers and dark terminal tail band. All birds recorded belong to the ssp. *L. a. smithsonianus*. **Voice** Mewing call *ki-auw* and harsh cackling noises *ca-ca-ca-ca*. **HH** Will appear along the coast but also on large freshwater ponds. Opportunistic feeder, taking fish but also visiting garbage dumps to look for scraps of food. **Status** Rare visitor from North America. Five records from Aruba and one from Bonaire, together with several unconfirmed sightings.

PLATE 31: GULLS III

Lesser Black-backed Gull *Larus fuscus* — L 55cm
Ar Meuwchi lomba preto chikito; **Bon**, **Cur** Not recorded; **NL** Kleine mantelmeeuw.
Quite like Great Black-backed Gull but smaller. Back and upper wings *dark grey rather than black*, *feet yellow*. Eyes yellow with red eye-ring. Bill yellow with red spot at tip. Juvenile indistinguishable from juvenile Herring Gull. In subsequent years immature Lesser Black-backed will grow progressively darker above. In first year has pinkish legs which turn more yellowish in second year. It has a gentler appearance than the Herring Gull due to rounded head with smaller bill. **Voice** Mewing *ki-auw* but lower and more nasal than in Herring Gull. **HH** Found along the coast but also on freshwater ponds. **Status** Rare visitor from North America. Eight records are known, all from Aruba.

Great Black-backed Gull *Larus marinus* — L 75cm
Ar Meuwchi lomba preto grandi; **Bon** Kahela lomba pretu; **Cur** Not recorded; **NL** Grote mantelmeeuw.
Largest gull. White with *black back and wings*. White spots at wingtips. Strong yellow bill with red spot. *Flesh-coloured feet*. Immature mottled brown and white above, underparts whitish. First-year has black bill and black tail band. Size alone and heavy flight with slow, deep wingbeats should separate immature from similar species like Herring Gull. It takes four years to attain adult plumage with brown feathers on the upper wings the last ones to disappear. **Voice** A deep and hoarse *eowk*. **HH** Usually single. Seen along the coast and will visit inner bays. **Status** Rare visitor from North America. Two records from birds in almost fully adult plumage from Aruba and one from Bonaire.

PLATE 32: TERNS I

Large-billed Tern *Phaetusa simplex* L 38cm
Ar Stèrnchi pico grandi; **Bon, Cur** Not recorded; **NL** Grootsnavelstern.
Immediately recognisable by its *huge yellow bill and striking black and white wing pattern*. Crown black, back and tail dark grey. Tail short and only slightly forked. Legs olive. In non-breeding plumage forehead and crown spotted with white. Immature with brown upperparts and tail tipped brown. **Voice** Utters a loud call similar to that of Laughing Gull but much shriller. Also a reedy *kaay-rak* and a nasal *ink-onk*. **HH** More attracted to a freshwater environment than other terns. Usually found along river banks, estuaries and lagoons. **Status** Rare visitor from South America. One old record on Aruba.

Royal Tern *Thalasseus maxima* L 50cm
Ar Stèrnchi di rey; **Bon, Cur** Meuchi real; **NL** Koningsstern.
Large tern with stout, *orange bill*. Black cap ends in an untidy crest, not cropped as in Caspian Tern. Tail deeply forked, on underwings the wingtips more dark grey with only tips blackish. Legs blackish. Outside breeding season *forehead and part of crown white*, unlike Caspian Tern. Immature with faintly greyish-brown upperparts and shorter tail. Bill and legs yellowish. Breeding birds belong to ssp. *T. m. maxima*. **Voice** Very high-pitched and thin *kreeee*, especially when competing for food with conspecifics. **HH** Coastal bird where it will rest on buoys, rocks and other obstacles jutting from sea surface. Plunge-dives after fish. Will follow fishing boats to forage for offal. **Status** Breeding bird and regular visitor. Breeding recorded for all three islands but not for every year. In winter migrants from North America visit.

Caspian Tern *Hydroprogne caspia* L 55cm
Ar Stèrnchi gigante; **Bon, Cur** Meuchi gigante; **NL** Reuzenstern.
Because of its size, can only be confused with Royal Tern. Larger and heavier than the latter, with large head and long, heavy *red bill with a black and orange tip*. Primaries show more black at the underside of the wing. In summer black cap and short, cropped crest gives an angular look to the head. In winter *cap, including forehead, is streaked white*. Tail short and not deeply forked. Overall more gull-like than Royal Tern. **Voice** A raucous, crow-like *kaah, kaah, kaah*. Also a shorter *kow*. **HH** Coastal bird but may also be found in freshwater ponds. Mixes with flocks of other terns and gulls. **Status** Rare visitor from North America. Only two records from Aruba, two from Bonaire and two from Curaçao. May be overlooked or confused with Royal Tern though.

PLATE 33: TERNS II

Gull-billed Tern *Gelochelidon nilotica* — L 35cm
Ar Stèrnchi haridó; **Bon**, **Cur** Meuchi haridó; **NL** Lachstern.
Unlike most sea terns, Gull-billed has a **short, only slightly forked tail**. Generally looks rather gull-like, with **thick, black bill**. Gives a white impression apart from black cap and striking black and white wing pattern. In winter the forehead is white, with the cap more brownish. Immature mottled brown on crown and back. Visiting birds belong to ssp. *S. n. aranea*. The presence of the Brazilian *S. n. groenvoldi* cannot be excluded but as in the field the two ssps are not separable, no records exist. **Voice** A variety of harsh and sharp notes *kay-ek, kay-ek*, staccato *kek-kek-kek* and softer, nasal *gek-gek*. **HH** Coastal bird. Usually single even when mixing with other terns. Will pick up food in flight varying from insects on land to small fish at sea. **Status** Irregular visitor from North America. Never very numerous but recorded during most of the year. Recorded from all three islands.

Cabot's Tern *Thalasseus acuflavidus* — L 42cm
Ar Stèrnchi grande; **Bon**, **Cur** Bubi chikí; **NL** Grote stern.
White tern with, during the breeding season, **black cap ending in small crest**. Colour of bill variable. Most birds on the islands have **yellow bill**, a form known as **Cayenne Tern**. Others have base or even the whole bill black with only the tip being yellow. Although there is considerable variation in bill colour, all South American birds are classed as Cayenne Tern *T. a. eurygnatha*. **During most of the year birds show white forehead and crown**. Immature upperparts mottled dusky brown. **Voice** A harsh and penetrating *karr-rick*. **HH** Found along the coast and large inner bays. Joins flocks of other seabirds out at sea. Plunge-dives for fish but can also snatch fish from surface when skimming the waves. **Status** Breeding has been reported from all three islands. Breeds in large colonies with nests close together. Most numerous between March and October. **Note** Both forms were previously treated as conspecific with Sandwich Tern *T. sandvicensis* of the Old World.

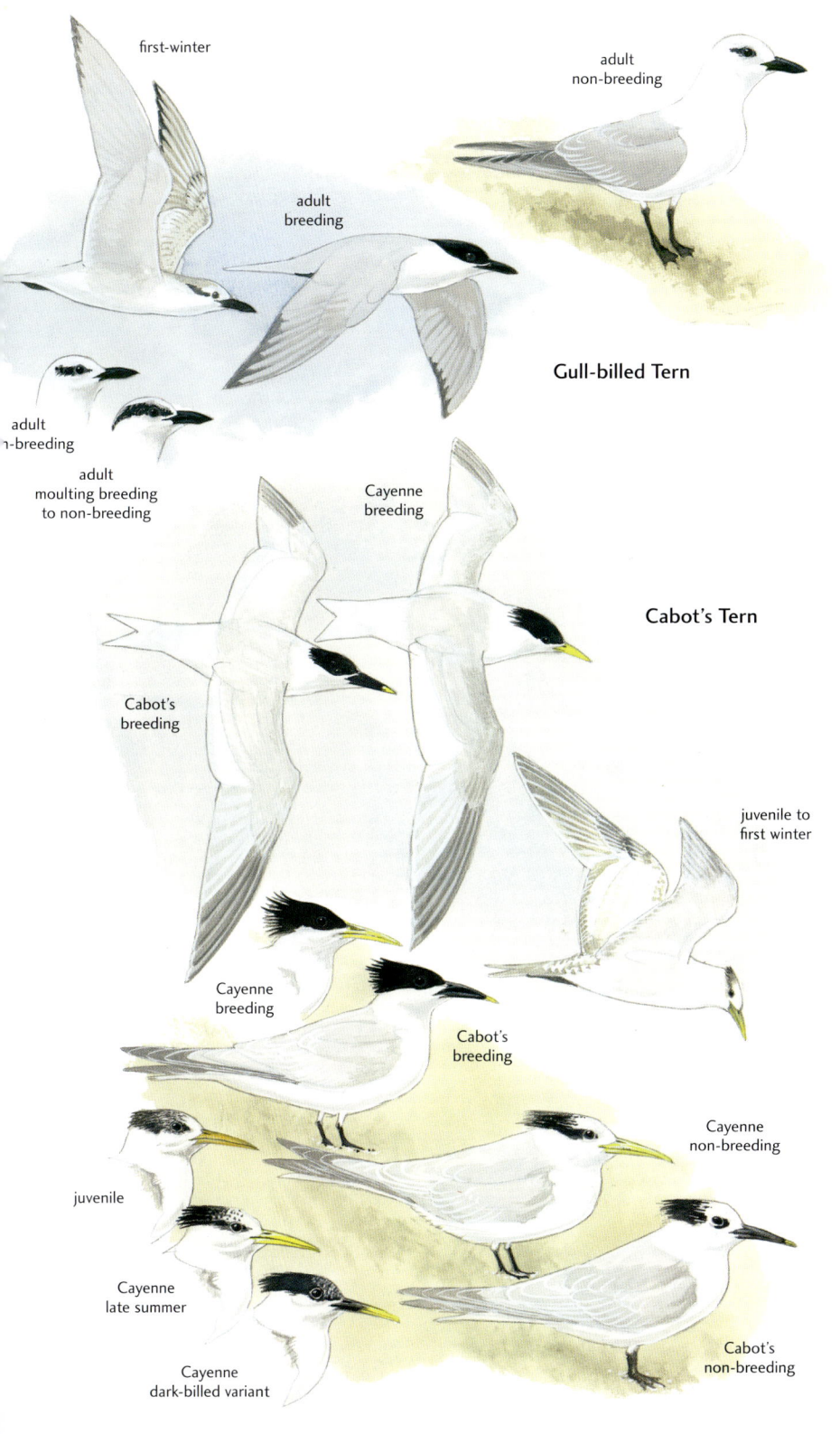

PLATE 34: TERNS III

Black Tern *Chlidonias niger* — L 24cm
Ar Stèrnchi preto; **Bon, Cur** Meuchi pretu; **NL** Zwarte stern.
Slightly larger than Least Tern but tail only slightly forked. Black bill. In summer plumage only tern with **black head, breast and belly and white underwings and undertail feathers**. Back, wings and tail dark grey. In winter underparts and head completely white except for hind part of crown and patch behind eye. Also black smudge at side of breast. Intermediate plumage always recognisable by pied pattern of black and white. Visiting birds are of ssp. *C. n. surinamensis*. **Voice** Usually silent but gives a shrill *kik, kik, kik*. **HH** Seen along the coast but also in inner bays and on freshwater ponds. **Status** Rare visitor. Known from seven records on Aruba, three on Bonaire and one from Curaçao.

Common Tern *Sterna hirundo* — L 35cm
Ar Stèrnchi comun; **Bon, Cur** Meuchi pik kòrá; **NL** Visdief.
Light grey-and-white tern with deeply forked, **dark-edged tail**. **Orange-red bill with black tip is determining feature**. Shows black flashes of wingtips in flight. **From below dark primaries enclose only small light wedg**e. Legs orange-red. In winter forehead and crown white, bill black. Leading edges of wings blackish. Bill brown-black, legs dull red. At rest wings extend to or beyond tip of tail. Immature like winter plumage but upperparts mottled brown and tail shorter. Island birds belong to ssp. *S. h. hirundo*. **Voice** High and penetrating *kree-eet* and a rasping alarm call *kee-aarrr*. **HH** Occurs along the coast but also in inner bays and salt pans. Hovers in the air with tail spread out and turned down. **Status** Breeding bird and regular visitor. Breeds on reef islands, dams in salt pans and islets in inner bays. Most numerous between April and November. In winter is joined by birds from North America.

Least Tern *Sternula antillarum* — L 22cm
Ar Stèrnchi chikito; **Bon, Cur** Meuchi chikitu; **NL** Amerikaanse dwergstern.
Smallest tern on the islands. Greyish-white with **white forehead** in all plumages, pale grey below. Bill yellow with black tip. Outer two primaries dark, conspicuous in flight. In winter plumage crown is mottled brown with a dark band running through the eye and around the head. The ssp. breeding on the islands is the nominate. The ssp. *S. a athalassos* may occur here, though so far there are no records available. It is whiter below and has an all-yellow bill. Juveniles and non-breeding adults of the two ssp. are practically inseparable. No definite records of the Yellow-billed Tern (*S. superciliaris*) exist yet. This species is slightly larger and with more black on the primaries than Least Tern but otherwise very similar. **Voice** High, chirpy and penetrating *cherrree-cherrree* and shorter *cheep*. **HH** Flight erratic and in breeding season attacks any intruder. Often hovers before plunging into the water. Found along the coast but also in salt pans. **Status** Breeding bird. Breeds in loose colonies on coastal rocks, sandy beaches and on dams in salt pans. Most numerous between April and September.

Roseate Tern *Sterna dougallii* — L 38cm
Ar Stèrnchi pecho ros; **Bon, Cur** Meuchi pechu ros; **NL** Dougall's stern.
Often overlooked due to similarity to Common Tern. *Generally whiter than latter species, has longer tail without dark edges. At rest wings do not reach tip of tail.* Bill black with variable amount of red at the base in breeding plumage. When breeding may show pink hue on breast. *In flight only outermost tip of wing shows some black and from below whole trailing edge is white*. In winter much like Common Tern but no dark edge on fore-edge of wing. Island birds belong to ssp. *S. d. dougallii*. **Voice** Different from Common Tern. Soft two-syllabic tones *chew-eeh*. Rasping alarm call *kaa-aag* and when attacking intruders *kee-eet*. **HH** Coastal bird which forages at sea. **Status** Breeding bird. Breeds on reef islands, in inner bays, lagoons and salt pans. Most numerous from April to August.

PLATE 35: PELAGIC TERNS

Sooty Tern *Onychoprion fuscatus*   L 40cm
Ar Stèrnchi bata preto; **Bon** Stèrnchi bata pretu; **Cur** Meuchi bachi pretu; **NL** Bonte stern.
Uniformly sooty black above, white below. *Only outer edges of tail white and white of forehead ends above the eye.* Bill black. Underwing white except for blackish tips of outermost primaries. Immature dull brown all over which makes it look like young Brown Noddy, but is the only all-dark tern with a deeply forked tail. Back spotted with white. Island birds belong to nominate ssp. **Voice** A loud three to four-syllable call *te-we-da-way* heard day and night. Also a yelping *wide-a-wake*. **HH** Much more pelagic than Bridled Tern and most often seen well off the coast. Seen on the islands only when nesting, between April and August. Gathers in flocks. Mixes with other seabirds but stands out as it does not plunge-dive for fish. **Status** Breeding bird. Breeding only known from reef islands on Aruba. Visitor on other islands.

Bridled Tern *Onychoprion anaethetus*   L 35cm
Ar Stèrnchi bril; **Bon**, **Cur** Meuchi brel; **NL** Brilstern.
One of the 'black-and-white' terns. Dark grey-brown above but back and tail lighter than upper wings. *White of forehead extends as a line to behind the eye. Outer tail feathers extensively white.* Hind neck lighter than either cap or mantle, almost forming a white collar. All these features distinguish it from Sooty Tern. Bill black. Underwing white. Immature mottled brown above and white below. Island birds belong to the West Indian ssp. *S. a. melanoptera*. **Voice** Different from Sooty Tern. A rather soft *hurrry-up*, also a yapping *wap-wap*. Alarm call a low but loud *karr-karr*. **HH** Pelagic in habits. Does not fly high but skims the waves which makes it difficult to observe. Does not gather in flocks but mixes with other seabirds. **Status** Breeding bird. Breeding known only from the reef islands on Aruba. Visitor to other two islands. Seen at sea between Aruba and the Paraguana peninsula and south of Bonaire.

Black Noddy *Anous minutus*   L 33cm
Ar Noddy preto; **Bon** Noddy pretu; **Cur** Not recorded; **NL** Witkapnoddy.
Smaller and darker than Brown Noddy. *White cap sharply separated from dark sides of head in straight line. White crown more sharply separated from black on neck than in Brown Noddy.* Bill black, longer and thinner than in Brown Noddy. Tail wedge-shaped with a small notch in the middle. Very difficult to tell the two species apart when not seen together. Black Noddy may impart a more uniformly black impression than Brown Noddy with a contrast between black back and paler tail. Birds on the islands belong to ssp. *A. m. americanus*. **Voice** In breeding colonies high-pitched cries, cackles and a staccato rattle but at sea mostly silent. **HH** Pelagic bird, forming large flocks following shoals of fish. Rather fluttering flight. **Status** Breeding bird. Breeds irregularly on reef islands off the coast of Aruba, otherwise only four records from Bonaire.

Brown Noddy *Anous stolidus*   L 38cm
Ar, **Bon**, **Cur** Noddy brúin; **NL** Noddy.
The two noddies which occur on the islands can be distinguished by the intensity of their colour. The Brown Noddy is *dark brown all over with a white crown which gradually changes to brown on the neck. White of forehead separated from brown in front of eye by curved, not straight line.* White line under eye. Tail wedge-shaped with a small notch in the middle. Bill and legs black. Local birds are of nominate ssp. **Voice** A harsh, crow-like *karr*, quite different from the penetrating calls of terns. **HH** Seen at sea in large numbers, skimming the waves. Tends to rest on rocky promontories at the northern tips of the islands. **Status** Breeding bird. Breeds irregularly on the reef islands of Aruba. Visitor on other islands.

PLATE 36: BLACK SKIMMER

Black Skimmer *Rynchops niger*   L 46cm
Ar Pico di skèr; **Bon**, **Cur** Bok'i skèr; **NL** Amerikaanse schaarbek.
Unmistakable when it literally ploughs the water with its lower mandible. As this causes considerable traction the bird has developed unusually long wings. Plumage black above and white below. Red bill with large black tip, **lower mandible longer than upper**. In non-breeding plumage has a white collar. Immature browner. The birds recorded on the islands probably belong to the South American ssp. *R. n. cinerascens* which has darkish underwings, an all-dark tail and narrow white trailing edge to the secondaries. The North American nominate ssp. is the smallest of the three ssp., with mostly white underwings and white tail with only the central pair of tail feathers black. A third ssp. from south-eastern South America, *R. n. intercedens*, is the largest of the three. It shows a broad white trailing edge to the secondaries. The tail is dark but every tail-feather has a white outer edge. **Voice** In flight a nasal bark *cuaa*. **HH** Found along the coast in shallow reef waters and on large freshwater ponds. **Status** Regular visitor. Recorded on all three islands, most numerous on Aruba.

Black Skimmer

PLATE 37: PIGEONS AND DOVES

Rock Pigeon *Columba livia* L 30cm
Ar Paloma comun; **Bon**, **Cur** Palomba; **NL** Rotsduif.
This is the common domestic pigeon found in all urban areas. The typical plumage is bluish with two black wingbars, a white rump and a broad black band at the tail tip. However, many other colour forms occur, with varied patterns in black, white, grey and red-brown. **Voice** A soft crooning *coo-coo*. When courting a very loud, far-reaching *coorrrooocoo*. **HH** Found everywhere near buildings where it nests on ledges and in crevices. Feeds on the ground wherever food remains may be found. In urban areas often almost underfoot. **Status** Breeding bird. Found on all three islands.

Eared Dove *Zenaida auriculata* L 25cm
Ar, **Bon**, **Cur** Buladeifi; **NL** Geoorde treurduif.
Medium-sized dove recognisable by **black spots on wings and behind eyes**. Upperparts pale brown, underparts with a pinkish sheen. **Terminal tail band rufous, not white** as in White-tipped Dove. Overall darker and browner than latter species. Red feet. Female duller in colour. Imm looks quite different, grey-brown all over with regular light barring. Island birds belong to the endemic ssp. *Z. a. vinacearufa*, distinguished by rufous tips to tail feathers, paler plumage and white chin. **Voice** A subdued low-pitched cooing. **HH** Bird of the countryside, visits urban areas only when food is scarce. When disturbed it will fly straight up, as if jumping, and immediately disappear again between the branches of nearby bushes. Feeds on various seeds. **Status** Breeding bird. Quite common on all three islands.

Bare-eyed Pigeon *Patagioenas corensis* L 34cm
Ar, **Cur** Ala blanca; **Bon** Palomba di mondi; **NL** Naaktoogduif.
White band across wings is most conspicuous feature. Bare skin around eye is light blue, surrounded by a black ring which gives the bird a spectacled look. Mainly greyish-brown with hints of pink, especially on the neck which may give it a scaled appearance. Bill whitish. Red legs and feet. Immature more brownish, especially on head and neck. **Voice** High, unmusical *roo-coo*, voice often breaking in mid-song. **HH** Formerly a bird of the countryside but now found in urban areas as well. When disturbed will fly off with loud clapping of wings. Feeds on all kinds of fruit and seeds. **Status** Breeding bird. Quite common on all three islands. Apparently there is much migration between the islands and the coast of Venezuela.

Scaly-naped Pigeon *Patagioenas squamosa* L 37cm
Ar Paloma azul; **Bon** Palomba pretu; **Cur** Blauduif; **NL** Roodhalsduif.
Largest pigeon on the islands. Dark greyish-blue **with purplish neck and scaled appearance of hind-neck spreading to the mantle**. Eyes red with buff eye-ring (yellowish in immature). Bill, legs and feet red. Female less purple with less scaling, greyer breast. Immature more brownish plumage and duller than adult. In the field often appears all dark but size should give it away. **Voice** Utters a deep resonant *roo-coo-coo-roooo*. **HH** Tends to keep to wooded hillsides but may swarm out over the island in search of fresh water, especially in dry years. Feeds on tree fruit and seeds. **Status** Breeding bird. Considered extinct on Aruba, common on Bonaire and scarce on Curaçao.

PLATE 38: DOVES

Common Ground Dove *Columbina passerina*
Ar Totolica; **Bon**, **Cur** Totolika; **NL** Musduif.   L 15cm
Most common and smallest of the doves on the islands. Male purplish-brown with iridescence on head and breast. Dark centers of head and breast feathers give the bird a *scaly appearance*. Eye red with blue-grey eye-ring. Bill orange with black tip, legs orange-pink. Female and juvenile plainer brown without the iridescent sheen. Numerous black spots on wings. Local birds belong to ssp. *C. p. albivitta* from northern South America and offshore islands. **Voice** An amazingly loud two-syllable *whoo-oop*. **HH** Very terrestrial, even when disturbed will rather walk away then take flight. Very common on all three islands, in countryside as well as in urban areas. Feeds on seeds of weeds and grasses. Nests are flimsy structures in thorny trees. When approached, birds may show injured-wing display to distract the intruder. **Status** Breeding bird on all three islands.

Ruddy Ground Dove *Columbina talpacoti*
Ar, **Cur** Not recorded; **Bon** Totolika venesolano; **NL** Steenduif.   L 17cm
Resembles Common Ground Dove but noticeably larger and *lacks scaly appearance of head and breast*. Overall more reddish-brown and in male the grey head contrasts with the rest of the body. Eyes red with grey eye-ring. Bill grey, legs pinkish. Female more greyish-brown, resembling female Common Ground Dove but lacks scaled breast. In flight distinguishable by black band on underwing. Immature dull brown with paler spots on wings. **Voice** A repeated *oo-oo-oo-oo*, rather monotonous. **HH** Terrestrial in habits, will readily visit urban areas. Feeds on small grass and weed seeds. **Status** Rare visitor from South America. One record on Bonaire, possibly blown in by a hurricane.

White-tipped Dove *Leptotila verreauxi*
Ar Pecho blanco; **Bon** Yiwiri; **Cur** Ala duru; **NL** Verraux' duif.   L 29cm
Larger and plumper than Eared Dove, with no conspicuous markings. Greyish-brown upperparts with lighter, vinaceous underparts. Head and neck vinaceous. Eye yellow with light blue eye-ring. *Tail with a white margin*, conspicuous when taking flight. Overall lighter in colour than Eared Dove. Red feet. Immature browner, especially on underparts. Local birds belong to ssp. *L. v. verreauxi* from northern South America and offshore islands. **Voice** A sultry, crooning, almost owl-like *ooo-ooo*, falling in pitch giving it a two-toned quality. **HH** Warier than other doves and when fleeing, with strong wing-clapping, will often land in nearby branch to take a better look at the intruder, bobbing head and tail. Inhabits dense undergrowth. **Status** Breeding bird. Common on all three islands.

PLATE 39: PARROTS I

Brown-throated Parakeet *Aratinga pertinax*   L 26cm
Ar, Bon, Cur Prikichi; NL Maisparkiet.
Mainly green with brownish head and throat. Each island has its own endemic ssp, which vary by **the amount of yellow on the head**. On Aruba the parakeet has at the most a little yellow near the eye (*A. p. arubensis*). On Curaçao the sides of the head show variable amounts of yellow but the crown is always green (nominate). Birds on Bonaire have the whole head yellow, including crown and sometimes neck (*A. p. xanthogenia*). The introduction of birds from one island to another has caused some mixing of the ssp., particularly on Aruba. **Voice** In flight a constant harsh, high-pitched shrieking. When feeding a constant chattering interspersed with shrieks. **HH** Occurs throughout the islands, making its presence known by loud harsh cries. Nests are often made in termites' nests. Feeds on all kinds of fruits including cactus fruits and seeds of the mesquite and cossie trees. **Status** Breeding bird. Common on all three islands.

Red-lored Parrot *Amazona autumnalis*   L 33cm
Ar, Bon Not recorded; Cur Lora frente korá; NL Geelwangamazone.
Typical all-green *Amazona* parrot with **red forehead and lores**. **Red speculum** in secondaries conspicuous in flight. Wing bend without any coloured patch. Green crown feathers scaled with a hint of lilac blue. Eyes appear orange, bill dusky. Has longer tail than Yellow-crowned Amazon. **Voice** At a distance best told by voice which is shriller than in other *Amazona* species, *chirak-chirak* and *oorak-oorak*. **HH** Bird of wooded areas. Will keep still when spotting an intruder. Often in mixed flocks with other amazon parrots. **Status** Introduced species. Originally from South America. No breeding has been reported as yet. Occurs only on Curaçao.

Yellow-crowned Parrot *Amazona ochrocephala*   L 36cm
Ar, Bon Not recorded; Cur Lora real; NL Geelvoorhoofdamazone.
Green all over with large yellow crown patch of variable extent. Bend of wing with red patch, and **red speculum** on secondaries. Tail yellowish on outer half, yellowish thighs. Outer tail feathers with red base but not visible in field. Eyes yellow with grey orbital skin. **Voice** A loud hoarse *currouw*. **HH** Bird of woodland. Rather silent but when flushed wings make clapping sound. **Status** Introduced species. Very popular cage bird as it mimics human sounds quite well. Occasionally nests have been found. Originally from South America, it has established itself on Curaçao.

Yellow-shouldered Parrot *Amazona barbadensis*   L 35cm
Ar, Bon, Cur Lora; NL Geelvleugelamazone.
The only parrot native to the islands. Big, rather plump bird, mainly green with yellow face. The **wing bend is yellow with red on the inside and it has a red speculum** which sets it apart from other (escaped) parrots (see 'escaped cage birds'). Throat and malar area may have a bluish sheen. There are indications that the birds from Bonaire and Blanquilla (Ven.) are heavier built than birds from the mainland but so far no sufficient scientific data are available to determine whether there is a significant difference. **Voice** Very harsh and throaty calls without any whistled notes. **HH** Bird of xerophytic woodlands. Will readily visit plantations when fruit, e.g. mangos, are ripe. Otherwise rather secretive, being active mainly in early morning and late afternoon. **Status** Breeding bird. Extinct on Aruba. Small population on Bonaire under constant threat from bird catchers. Since a tropical storm passed in 1988, has been present on Curaçao where it apparently breeds. It is not known if these birds were blown over from Bonaire or if they escaped from cages.

Orange-winged Parrot *Amazona amazonica*   L 33cm
Ar, Cur Lora ala oraño; Bon Not recorded; NL Oranjevleugelamazone.
Green all over with yellow crown patch surrounded by blue circle, yellow cheeks. Wing bend green, **orange speculum** on secondaries. Outer tail feathers tipped yellow. Eyes orange-yellow, bill pale with darker tip. Undertail orange with green band. **Voice** High and screechy, sounding like *c'm-quick,c'm-quick*. **HH** In wooded areas, dry shrubs but will also visit urban areas. Will visit cultivated fruit trees. **Status** Introduced species. No nesting has been reported as yet. Originally from South America. Occurs on Aruba and Curaçao.

PLATE 40: PARROTS II

Rose-ringed Parakeet *Psittacula krameri* L 42cm
Ar, **Bon** Not recorded; **Cur** Prikichi renchi ros; **NL** Halsbandparkiet.
Large all-green parakeet with long, very pointed tail. Its main feature is the *light to dark red thick bill*. Male has bluish nape with reddish feathers encircling it, difficult to see as often covered by green head feathers. **Voice** Less hoarse than of other parakeets, more like a high whistle. **HH** Wooded areas, especially near plantations with fruit trees. **Status** Introduced species. Originally from south-east Asia, it has established itself on Curaçao. A small breeding population has established itself near Piscadera and Julianadorp. Suffers high mortality in very dry years.

Chestnut-fronted Macaw *Ara severus* L 48cm
Ar, **Cur** Wakamaya chiki; **Bon** Not recorded; **NL** Dwergara.
Small macaw, immediately recognisable in flight by its *red underwings and undertail*. Mainly green with blue crown. Facial skin whitish. Primaries blue. Rose-ringed Parakeet is smaller and completely green including undersides of wings and tail. Rapid wingbeats distinguish it from other, larger macaws. **Voice** Utters loud, hoarse cries in flight. Pairs may participate in parrot-like song with gurgling, chattery noises. **HH** Usually in pairs. May gather in large groups at nightfall at fixed roosting sites. **Status** Introduced species. Breeding has been recorded. Originally from South America. It is present on Aruba and Curaçao.

Green-rumped Parrotlet *Forpus passerinus* L 14cm
Ar, **Bon** Not recorded; **Cur** Bibitu; **NL** Groene muspapegaai.
Very small, green parrot. In male *upper- and underwing-coverts and primary coverts are blue*. However, in the field this blue is difficult to see. Eyes brown with grey eyelids. Bill pale ivory. Female all green with paler forehead, sometimes yellowish. **Voice** In flight a clear, rather jubilant *chit-it, chit-it*. When feeding maintains a constant chatter. **HH** Low tree and shrub vegetation where its unending chatter makes it easy to find. **Status** Uncertain. Thought to have been introduced from South America as a cage bird but exhausted specimens have been found which may mean migration from the mainland. Very irregular in appearance. A small population existed on Malpais, Curaçao, in the 1960s and 1970s but seems to have disappeared by the 1980s. Not reported from the other islands.

Scarlet-fronted Parakeet *Aratinga wagleri* L 34cm
Ar, **Bon** Not recorded; **Cur** Prikichi frente kòrá; **NL** Wagler's parkiet.
Green all over with *forehead bright red*. May show traces of red on neck, breast and bend of wing. Bill brownish; Rose-ringed Parakeet has red bill. Eye orange to yellow with pale ring. Underwing and undertail yellowish-green. **Voice** Very vociferous, constantly screeching loudly when in flight, quite unlike Blue-crowned Parakeet. **HH** Wooded areas. Always moves in large, noisy flocks. Feeds on fruits and seeds. **Status** Introduced species. Originally from South America. It has established itself on Curaçao.

Blue-crowned Parakeet *Aratinga acuticaudata* L 34cm
Ar, **Bon** Not recorded; **Cur** Prikichi kabes blou; **NL** Blauwkoparatinga.
Large parakeet, completely green with long pointed tail. Forecrown blue. Yellow-orange eyes with conspicuous whitish ring. Outer tail feathers dull red on inner webs but difficult to see. Bill whitish; Rose-ringed Parakeet has red bill. Underwings and undertail yellowish-green. **Voice** In flight a babbling *crwa-crwa-crwa*, a lot less harsh than in Scarlet-fronted Parakeet. **HH** In wooded areas and xerophytic shrub. Feeds on fruits and seeds, also when they are on the ground. **Status** Introduced species. Originally from South America. No breeding has been reported as yet. Occurs only on Curaçao.

PLATE 41: CUCKOOS

Yellow-billed Cuckoo *Coccyzus americanus* — L 30cm
Ar Cucu pico hel; **Bon**, **Cur** Kuku pik hel; **NL** Geelsnavelkoekoek.
Stands out by its rather laborious flight, 'dragging along' a long tail when crossing a road for example. Above brown, below grey to white. In flight rufous in wings is conspicuous. *Tail with conspicuous white 'flags'*. Lower mandible yellow, upper mandible black. Conspicuous *yellow eye-ring*. Difficult to observe when not moving as it will sit almost motionless in trees and shrubs. **Voice** Mostly silent during migration. Otherwise utters repeated *ka... ka...* and also a slow descending cooing. **HH** Any habitat with trees, like mangroves, fruit tree stands, xerophytic shrub. Moves quietly among the branches to look for caterpillars, insects and even small lizards. Readily visits gardens. **Status** Regular visitor from North America. Passes the islands en route to South America on winter migration. Often arrives completely exhausted and is easy to approach.

Mangrove Cuckoo *Coccyzus minor* — L 30cm
Ar Cucu mangel; **Bon**, **Cur** Kuku mangel; **NL** Mangrovekoekoek.
Similar to Yellow-billed Cuckoo but pale morph is *buff, not white, below with no brown on upperparts*. Dark morph is *dark cinnamon* below. Bill black with only the base of lower mandible yellow. Black patch behind eye. Tail feathers with same white spots as in Yellow-billed. May easily be confused with the (as yet unrecorded) Dark-billed Cuckoo (*C. melacoryphus*) from South America but the latter has no yellow on lower mandible and is more buff underneath. **Voice** Mostly silent during migration. Utters a hoarse *ke-ke-ke-ke* and a low *gawk, gawk, gawk*. **HH** Any habitat with trees and shrubs. Seems to feed mainly on large insects like locusts and caterpillars. Shows same behaviour as Yellow-billed. **Status** Irregular visitor from West Indies and Florida. May be seen throughout the year but never very numerous.

Grey-capped Cuckoo *Coccyzus lansbergi* — L 25cm
Ar, **Cur** Not recorded; **Bon** Kuku kabes shinishi; **NL** Grijskopkoekoek.
Smallest of the cuckoos to be encountered on the islands. Dark, reddish-brown above and dark buff below. *Slate-grey cap contrasts with rest of plumage*. Bill black. Eye dark brown with grey eye-ring. Legs grey. Tail-feathers with conspicuous white spots. Immature has brown cap. **Voice** Rather silent. Utters a fast repeated *cucucucucu*. **HH** Very secretive habits, keeping hidden between thick foliage in low vegetation. **Status** Rare visitor from South America. One record on Bonaire.

Groove-billed Ani *Crotophaga sulcirostris* — L 30cm
Ar Chuchubi preto; **Bon**, **Cur** Chuchubi pretu; **NL** Groefsnavelani.
Completely black with long tail and short wings. Flight looks laborious, prefers to glide from one tree to the next, when spread-out tail is very conspicuous. Bill black, high-arched, with grooves and ridges. Eyes brown. **Voice** Very noisy, uttering high-pitched, hissing cries *pssseeee*. **HH** Always lives in groups. Numerous in wet years but tends to crowd around places with farm animals in dry periods. Builds communal nests, used by more than one female. Omnivorous, feeds on all kinds of insects and even lizards but also on fruits and seeds. **Status** Breeding bird. Breeding has been reported from all three islands.

Greater Ani *Crotophaga major* — L 48cm
Ar Chuchubi preto mayor; **Bon** Not recorded; **Cur** Chuchubi pretu grandi; **NL** Grote ani.
Very large and glossy bluish-black. *Large bill with distinct hump*. Yellow eye conspicuous in adult. Long tail which seems to move in all directions when bird is roosting. Immature with brown eyes. As with other anis, seems to move awkwardly, hopping and lunging for prey. **Voice** A variety of croaks and hisses. Typically a guttural *kro-koro* reminiscent of a boiling kettle. **HH** Often in small groups moving through low vegetation. Hops awkwardly on foliage looking for insects, caterpillars and small lizards. **Status** Rare visitor from South America. One record of a single bird on Aruba and one on Curaçao.

PLATE 42: OWLS AND OILBIRD

Barn Owl *Tyto alba* — L 29cm
Ar Not recorded; **Bon**, **Cur** Palabrua; **NL** Kerkuil.
Unless found at roost, usual view is of a white shape appearing in the beams of car headlights. Upperparts are mottled golden-brown, underparts white speckled with black. The heart-shaped face is typical. No ear tufts. Feathered legs and toes. The subspecies found on the islands (*T. a. bargei*) is among the smallest of this cosmopolitan species. One owl found on Bonaire could not be assigned to a definite race, showing a mix of characteristics. The race in adjacent Venezuela is *hellmayri*. **Voice** Makes a variety of hissing and scraping noises but seldom heard. Does not hoot. **HH** Nocturnal. Roosting places and nest sites include attics of old houses or churches, limestone caves and even vertical shafts of old mining activities. Hunts for rodents, bats and small birds. **Status** Breeds in small numbers. Breeding has been reported on Curaçao and Bonaire. Absent from Aruba.

Burrowing Owl *Athene cunicularia* — L 21cm
Ar, **Cur** Choco; **Bon** Not recorded; **NL** Holenuil.
Small, terrestrial owl which can easily be seen in daylight. Long-legged, pale brown above, spotted buff and white. Underside buff with brown spots. A very small breeding population exists on Aruba and has been assigned to a separate ssp. *A. c. arubensis*. It is slightly larger and paler than the ssp. of coastal Venezuela and Margarita, with fewer dark markings underneath. Conspicuous white supercilia above the large yellow eyes give the bird a look of constant amazement. **Voice** Utters two cooing notes heard through the night. **HH** Occurs in flat areas and between large boulders where it digs a burrow in sandy spots. In daytime, especially in the morning and early evening, the pair will often stand in front of the entrance to the burrow. **Status** Breeding bird on Aruba. Absent from the other two islands though once a straggler was sighted on Curaçao.

Oilbird *Steatornis caripensis* — L 45cm
Ar Para zeta; **Bon**, **Cur** Not recorded; **NL** Vetvogel.
Nocturnal bird which in daytime resides in caves. Looks like large nightjar. Rufous-brown above with rows of black-encircled white spots on upperside of wing and outer tail feathers. Bill strong and hooked, legs very short. **Voice** In flight a metallic *cree, cree, cree*. Various hisses and snoring sounds. Clicking sounds when in cave, used for echolocation. **HH** Inhabits deep caves, emerging from them when dusk falls amid loud screeches to search for fruit-bearing trees, sometimes flying large distances in one night. When it cannot reach its cave before dawn, it may rest out in the open. **Status** Rare visitor from South America. One record of a single bird on Aruba. Nearest known colony is in the Sierra de San Luis near Coro, Venezuela.

PLATE 43: NIGHTHAWKS

Antillean Nighthawk *Chordeiles gundlachii* L 24cm
Ar, **Bon** Not recorded; **Cur** Tapa kaminda antiano; **NL** Antilliaanse nachtzwaluw.
Very similar to Common Nighthawk. *Darker overall, white band across wing and white terminal tail band*. Male white throat, buff in female extending to behind the ear. In resting bird the *pale tertials* distinguish it from Common Nighthawk. *Wingtips do not extend to tip of tail* in roosting bird. **Voice** Insect-like *krity-krit-krit*; most certain way to distinguish from Common Nighthawk. **HH** Forages high over the tops of trees, open fields and urban areas. Performs deep dives chasing after insects. **Status** Rare visitor from Greater Antilles. Two records from Curaçao.

Lesser Nighthawk *Chordeiles acutipennis* L 20cm
Ar Not recorded; **Bon**, **Cur** Tapa kaminda menor; **NL** Texasnachtzwaluw.
Greyish-brown with white band across throat. *White bands near wingtip and tip of tail except on the central tail feathers*, both visible in flight. White crescent at either side of throat. As all nighthawks and nightjars difficult to identify as mostly seen only briefly when disturbed at night. At rest wingtips reach to tail tip but not beyond. *Female has buff wing bands* and lacks white band across tail. Both sexes of Common Nighthawk have more central white wing band. **Voice** A winnowing, trilling call when in flight. **HH** On migration flies quite high in plain daylight. Normally rests under bushes during the day and becomes active at nightfall. At night often sits on roads and flies straight up when caught in the headlights of a car. **Status** Rare visitor from South America. One record on Curaçao and one on Bonaire.

Common Nighthawk *Chordeiles minor* L 23cm
Ar Tapa camina amerikano; **Bon**, **Cur** Tapa kaminda merikano; **NL** Amerikaanse nachtzwaluw.
Somewhat larger than Lesser Nighthawk. More greyish overall. *White band across wing situated closer to wing 'wrist' than to tip in contrast with former species*. Throat white in male, buff in female, more extensive than in Lesser Nighthawk. Both sexes have white band across tail tip, broader than in Lesser Nighthawk. *At rest wingtips project beyond tip of tail*. Visiting birds assigned to the ssp. *C. m. minor* but other ssp. may occur as they all seem to winter in South America. **Voice** An insect-like buzz and a nasal *peernt*. **HH** During daytime rests lengthwise on branch. Flies high, also when foraging. Flies with deep wingbeats. **Status** Irregular visitor from North America and the Greater Antilles. Seen in broad daylight on high foraging flights, almost always in small flocks. Mostly seen during winter migration but also a July record from Bonaire.

PLATE 44: NIGHTJARS AND SWIFTS

White-tailed Nightjar *Caprimulgus cayennensis*   L 22cm
Ar Tapa camina; **Bon** Palabrua; **Cur** Para karpinté; **NL** Witstaartnachtzwaluw.
Most often seen as a pair of red eyes caught in car headlights at the side of the road, very often under lampposts. Conspicuous *cinnamon-coloured nuchal collar. Underparts white, white wing patch and tail mostly white from below*. Female smaller and lacks white markings. Because of the amount of white in the male, easily recognised when taking wing. Island birds belong to ssp. *C. c. insularis*, paler with more buff on upperparts than other ssp. **Voice** A whistling call *pee-cheeeuuw*. **HH** In daytime rests on ground under acacia trees or in opuntia shrubs. Becomes active well after dusk. During courtship claps wings together with an audible tapping sound. **Status** Breeding bird. Breeds on all three islands.

Chuck-will's-widow *Antrostomus carolinensis*   L 30cm
Ar Tapa camina viuda; **Bon, Cur** Tapa kaminda biuda; **NL** Chuck-will's-widow.
By far the largest nightjar to be encountered on the islands. Reddish-brown with greyish crown. Narrow *whitish collar across throat. No white bands across wings* which distinguishes it immediately from the other species of nighthawks and nightjars on the islands. Male has some white in tail but this is usually concealed. **Voice** Not heard in winter. Otherwise gives characteristic *chuck-willow-willah*. **HH** By day rests on ground in wooded areas, only seen when flushed. At night chases wildly after prey. **Status** Rare visitor from North America. One record from each of the three islands. **Note** Formerly placed in *Caprimulgus*.

Chimney Swift *Chaetura pelagica*   L 13cm
Ar, Bon, Cur Veloz di chimenea; **NL** Schoorsteengierzwaluw.
Large swift, gives an all black impression. Greyish-black all over, but not shiny. *Lighter on throat* and upper breast. *Short, stubby tail which makes it seem almost tail-less*. Wings narrower than in swallows. Almost always in small flocks high up in the air. **Voice** Twitters and chirps in flight. **HH** Congregates with other swifts and swallows especially during migration. **Status** Irregular visitor from North America. Seen in small numbers on Aruba during autumn migration. Two records each from Bonaire and Curaçao.

Black Swift *Cypseloides niger*   L 16cm
Ar, Bon Not recorded; **Cur** Veloz pretu; **NL** Zwarte gierzwaluw.
Larger than Chimney Swift and distinguished from the latter by *longer wings and slightly forked tail*. Sooty black with upperparts darker than underparts. Forehead whitish. Throat black, not lighter as in Chimney Swift. **Voice** A series of fast, rather hoarse chirps and chattering noises. **HH** Flight less erratic than in Chimney Swift; more gliding with fewer wingbeats. **Status** Rare visitor from Greater Antilles and possibly from North America. Only one record from Curaçao.

White-tailed Nightjar

Chuck-will's-widow

Black Swift

Chimney Swift

PLATE 45: HUMMINGBIRDS

Rufous-breasted Hermit *Glaucis hirsuta*   L 11cm
Ar, Bon Not recorded; Cur Blenchi pechu brùin; NL Roodborstheremietkolibrie.
Bronze-green above and rufous below. The typical hermit face pattern of a dark band through the eye bordered at both sides by lighter lines is barely developed in this species. Central tail feathers not elongated, green. Outer tail feathers chestnut-brown. Black band across tail-end and white tip. Female duller than male. **Voice** A shrill, squeaky *tseep*. Territorial song *tsee-tsee-tsee-tsee-tsee*, answered by female. **HH** Usually forages singly at lower elevations, often flying the same route for several days. **Status** Rare visitor from South America. One record from Curaçao.

Blue-tailed Emerald *Chlorostilbon mellisugus*   L 8cm
Ar, Bon, Cur Blenchi bèrdè; NL Blauwstaartsmaragdkolibrie.
Smaller and more common of the two resident hummingbirds on the islands. Male glittering green with steel-blue, slightly forked tail. Bill straight and black. Female duller, lighter green and grey below with white line behind the eye. When in rest a white, downy tuft of feathers may show at the base of the leg in both sexes. Birds on the islands belong to ssp. *C. m. caribaeus*, with just a hint of a bluish tinge on throat. **Voice** Song a thin, merry twittering. When chasing away competitors a harsh rattle. **HH** Confiding and can be observed in any garden with flowering plants. Several birds may visit the same flowering tree, with constant chasing and fighting. Tube-like flowers will often be pierced at the bottom to reach the nectar inside. **Status** Breeding bird. Breeds on all three islands.

White-necked Jacobin *Florisuga mellivora*   L 11cm
Ar Blenchi nèk blanco.; Bon Not recorded; Cur Blenchi nèk blanku; NL Witnekkolibrie.
Male shiny with blue head, throat and breast and bright green upperparts. Easily distinguished by its white belly, tail and white neck band. Central tail feathers green. Juvenile male shows bright rufous whiskers from base of bill to lower throat. Female green with underparts white, scaled with grey and green; variable in colour, may show some blue on throat. Immature duller. Female and immature have strongly barred undertail feathers. **Voice** A soft *tssit* when feeding. **HH** Tends to forage at higher levels in vegetation. Aggressive towards other species at flowering trees. Also takes small insects and spiders. Perches in the open on high twigs. **Status** Rare visitor from South America. One record from Aruba and one from Curaçao.

Ruby-topaz Hummingbird *Chrysolampis mosquitus*   L 10cm
Ar, Bon, Cur Dòrnasol; NL Muskietkolibrie.
When not in direct sunlight looks dark brown and only the *reddish-brown tail* will give away its identity. In sunlight the crown and nape turn glitteringly red (ruby) while the throat turns yellow (topaz). Changing light may reveal green and orange colours on the throat. The conical appearance of the head is also a good characteristic. Juvenile male has yellow on throat bordered by white. Female greyish-green with grey underparts but also with a reddish-brown tail. Broad black band at the end of the tail with just the tips of the tail feathers white. **Voice** A high squeaky *teerrt*. **HH** Tends to stay more in the bush than Blue-tailed Emerald. Will visit flowering trees and bushes, defending its food source aggressively against other flower-visiting birds. **Status** Breeding bird. Breeds on all three islands.

Rufous-breasted Hermit

Blue-tailed Emerald

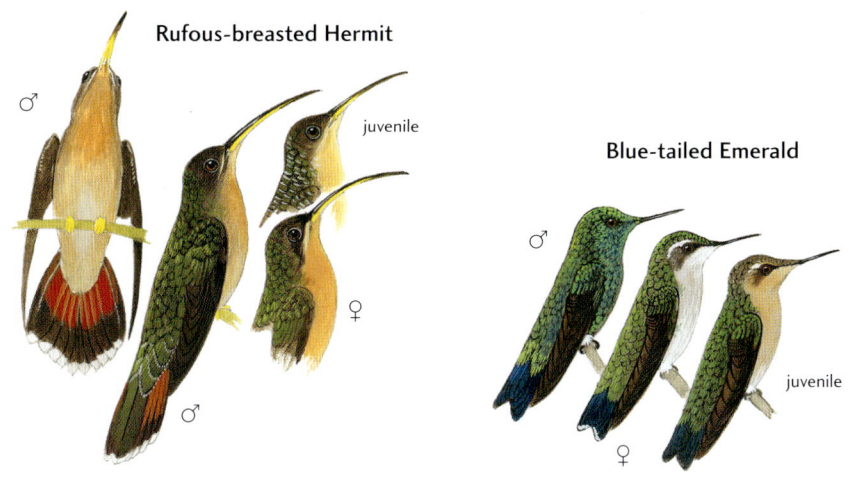

White-necked Jacobin

Ruby-topaz Hummingbird

PLATE 46: KINGFISHERS

Amazon Kingfisher *Chloroceryle amazona* L 29cm
Ar Cabez grandi bèrdè; **Bon**, **Cur** Not recorded; **NL** Amazoneijsvogel.
Green above with a white collar around the neck connected with white chin, throat and white belly. Male has a rufous breast-band while female has an incomplete spotty green band. The bill is disproportionately large. **Voice** When disturbed an annoyed *chak*. Song *qew-qew-qew-qew* in rapid succession. **HH** Found at the coast but also in freshwater ponds with fish. Sits on high perch from which it will dive down to catch fish. Sometimes hovers in the air before plunging down. **Status** Rare visitor from South America. One record on Aruba.

Ringed Kingfisher *Megaceryle torquata* L 38cm
Ar Cabez grandi barica còrá; **Bon** Not recorded; **Cur** Kabes grandi barika kòrá; **NL** Amerikaanse reuzenijsvogel.
Big kingfisher (much larger than Belted) with unkempt crest and large grey bill with orange patch near base of lower mandible. Male has *bluish-grey upperparts with white collar circling entire neck*. Small white spot in front of eye. Underparts chestnut-brown with white undertail-coverts. In flight conspicuous white patch at base of primaries. Female similar but shows *greyish chest band separated from chestnut underparts by white band*. Undertail-coverts also chestnut. Immature has brown chestband and shows white spots on wings. **Voice** In flight a loud *kek*, extended to a rattle *kekekekek* when disturbed. **HH** Along the coast and in freshwater ponds with fish. Hunts from a high perch, usually without hovering. **Status** Rare visitor from South America. Two records from Aruba and one from Curaçao.

Belted Kingfisher *Megaceryle alcyon* L 30cm
Ar Cabez grandi; **Bon**, **Cur** Kabes grandi; **NL** Bandijsvogel.
Unmistakable large bluish-grey bird with *white throat extending to neck-collar, white belly and bluish-grey breast band*. Very large head with bushy crest. Female similar to male but with an additional *rufous chest-band and rufous flanks*. Flight fast but laborious. Might be confused with Ringed Kingfisher but the latter is much larger and has chestnut underparts, not white. **Voice** A loud, cackling rattle, higher than in Ringed Kingfisher. **HH** Mostly seen along the coast sitting on bare branches or rocky promontories from where it will dive straight into shallow waters to get the fish. May hover before diving. **Status** Regular visitor from North America but never very numerous.

PLATE 47: SAPSUCKER AND FLYCATCHERS I

Yellow-bellied Sapsucker *Sphyrapicus varius* — L 21cm
Ar Parha carpinté barica hel; **Bon, Cur** Para karpinté barika hel; **NL** Geelbuiksapspecht.
Upperparts black with numerous white spots and dots. *Large white patches on the wings*. Red hood and throat patch in male are distinctive features. Underparts yellowish on flanks, more white on belly, heavily barred with black. Female has white throat. Immature more brown all over but with white wing patch. **Voice** Mostly silent in winter quarters. Alarm call *weetik-weetik*. In aggressive encounters with conspecifics a sharp *yuk-yuk-yuk*. **HH** Unlike woodpeckers, drills holes in the trunks of trees to get to the sap. Often drills several holes in a distinctive neat row. **Status** Rare visitor from North America. Eleven records from all three islands, all between October and the middle of January.

Small-billed Elaenia *Elaenia parvirostris* — L 15cm
Ar Elenia pico chikito; **Bon, Cur** Not recorded; **NL** Kortsnavelelenia.
The round crestless head and prominent whitish eye-ring distinguish this from the other *Elaenia* species reported from the islands. Upperparts olivaceous, breast grey and belly *whitish*. Two white wingbars and a vague third one. Bill has slightly pinkish hue. White crown patch, but mostly concealed. **Voice** Mostly silent. A subdued *pew* or *peewhew* most common call. **HH** Quite inconspicuous. Forages in lower levels of vegetation but moves quietly, which makes it difficult to spot. **Status** Rare visitor from South America. Known with certainty from only one record from Aruba but possibly overlooked.

Caribbean Elaenia *Elaenia martinica* — L 15cm
Ar Elenia caribe; **Bon** Chonchorogai; **Cur** Whimpie; **NL** Witbuikelenia.
Elaenias are notoriously difficult to identify. The Caribbean Elaenia is an unobtrusive little flycatcher, olive-grey above with light grey chest and belly with yellowish sheen. Two white wingbars and white edges to inner secondary flight feathers. White crown patch but can only be seen when bird raises its crest. Bill dark brown with lower mandible largely flesh-coloured. Lesser Elaenia is smaller and greener above with more yellow on belly. Islands' population belongs to ssp. *E. m. risii*, also found on the Virgin islands and Antigua. **Voice** Important in identification. Utters a rather loud whistle *pee-wee-pee-wee* and song *pee-wee-reereeree*. **HH** Even when singing difficult to observe as it stays hidden between foliage. Scrub and open wood. **Status** Breeding bird. Caribbean in distribution but the islands are the only known sites where they occur in the southern Caribbean. Breeding has been reported from all three islands but present status on Aruba uncertain.

Lesser Elaenia *Elaenia chiriquensis* — L 14cm
Ar Not recorded; **Bon, Cur** Elenia chikí; **NL** Kleine elenia
Difficult to distinguish from Caribbean Elaenia. *Paler and greener above, breast greyer and belly more yellowish*. Crest more prominent but often held flat giving the back of the head a square outline. White crown patch concealed but often visible from behind. Narrow white eye-ring. Two white wingbars more faded than in Caribbean Elaenia. Island records relate to *E. c. albivertex* – more greyish above and pale yellow below than other ssp. **Voice** Quite different from that of Caribbean Elaenia. A clear whistle *weééa*. **HH** Usually in mid-levels of dense vegetation, hides behind leaves, hence difficult to observe. Quieter than Caribbean Elaenia. **Status** Irregular visitor from South America, possibly resident. Two birds recorded on Curaçao and four records from Bonaire. Numerous unconfirmed observations of possible Lesser Elaenia including reports of nesting make status of bird uncertain.

Northern Scrub-Flycatcher *Sublegatus arenarum* — L 14cm
Ar Parha bobo; **Bon** Chonchorogai; **Cur** Para bobo; **NL** Noordelijke struikvliegenpikker.
Greenish-grey crested flycatcher with two whitish wingbars (in fresh plumage there is a vague third wingbar on the lesser wing-coverts) and light edges to inner wing feathers. Grey breast sharply divided from yellow belly. *Large eyes give it a very gentle expression*. Narrow white eye-ring with indistinct eye-stripe. Tail slightly forked and of a contrasting dusky hue. The sharp division between grey and yellow, the supercilium and the contrasting tail distinguish this species from *Elaenia* flycatchers. Belongs to the endemic ssp. *S. a. pallens*, distinguished by the pale pure grey breast and sulphur yellow underparts. **Voice** A burbling *peewééree*. **HH** Hides in bushes and acacia trees from which it may sally forth to catch flying insects, always returning to the same perch. **Status** Breeds on all three islands.

PLATE 48: FLYCATCHERS II

Olive-sided Flycatcher *Contopus cooperi*   L 18cm
Ar, **Cur** Not recorded; **Bon** Pibi canades; **NL** Sparrenpiewie.
Apart from its dark appearance and large size, this flycatcher is immediately recognisable by the **white tufts of feathers behind the wings when resting**. Plumage similar to Eastern Pewee but with much more contrast. Bill rather broad, lower mandible orange. Relatively short tail, large head with crest giving a flattened appearance to back of head. Flanks and sides of breast brownish with darker stripes. Median belly and up to throat bright white. **Voice** Mostly silent on wintering grounds. May occasionally give a whistled *pip-pip-pip*. **HH** Always solitary. Often perches on the highest twig in a tree or on protruding dead branches. Sallies forth after prey, returning to same perch. May use same perch for weeks, establishing a kind of feeding territory. **Status** Rare visitor from North America. Two records from Bonaire, both in May during spring migration.

Eastern Wood Pewee *Contopus virens*   L 15cm
Ar Pibi di este; **Bon** Pibi di ost; **Cur** Not recorded; **NL** Oostelijke bospiewie.
Dark olive-grey above with two light grey wingbars and lighter edges to inner wing feathers. Relatively large head with long bill, lower mandible yellowish with dark tip. Slight crest. No eye-ring. Belly whitish with median line going up the grey-olive breast. Undertail-coverts yellow. Its *dark overall colour* sets it apart from similar sized other flycatchers on the islands. **Voice** A whistled *peeeuh* and a longer plaintive *peeawee*. Both can be heard on the wintering grounds. **HH** Usually single. Perches on protruding twigs to sally forth after prey and subsequently returning to the same perch. Prefers rather dense vegetation. **Status** Rare visitor from North America. One record from Aruba and three from Bonaire.

Vermilion Flycatcher *Pyrocephalus rubinus*   L 13cm
Ar Pímpiri còrà; **Bon**, **Cur** Not recorded; **NL** Rode tiran.
Male unmistakable with bright black-and-red pattern. Female is ashy brown above, whitish below with dark streaks on breast, flanks and abdomen with pinkish hue. Immature male like female but may show patches of pink; breast to lower belly with lines of v-shaped spots. **Voice** A high metallic *peep* or a three-toned trill. Song of male *ti-ti-trr-e-e-E*. **HH** Most often found perching conspicuously on fence-posts, barbed wire or open branches. Often chases after flying insects near the ground. **Status** Rare visitor from South America. One record, an immature male, from Aruba.

Cattle Tyrant *Machetornis rixosus*   L 20cm
Ar Pímpiri vakero; **Bon**, **Cur** Not recorded; **NL** Veetiran.
Very terrestrial flycatcher. Light brown above, underparts bright yellow. Concealed bright red crown patch. Vague dusky stripe through conspicuous red eye. Looks somewhat like a kingbird but its habits make it easy to identify. **Voice** A high *pee-prree-prree*, similar to that of Tropical Kingbird but higher-pitched. **HH** Forages mainly on the ground where its long legs help it to run swiftly. Will follow cattle to pick up disturbed prey. **Status** Rare visitor from South America. One record from Aruba of one bird which stayed for almost a year.

Brown-crested Flycatcher *Myiarchus tyrannulus*   L 20cm
Ar, **Cur** Tirano grandi; **Bon** Chonchorogai; **NL** Cayennetiran.
Intermediate in size between Northern Scrub-flycatcher and Tropical Kingbird. Head brownish with a squared-off appearance due to slightly raised crest. *Rufous in wings and in uppertail-coverts diagnostic*. Bill large, slightly hooked at tip, black with lower mandible pinkish. Island birds belong to the ssp. *M. t. tyrannulus* from northern South America. **Voice** Loud rolling *pee-prrree*, song loud *wéé-wee-weerrr*. **HH** Bird of thorn scrub; prefers thorn trees in open places but does not choose exposed roosting places. **Status** Breeding bird. Breeds on all three islands but not very common on Aruba.

PLATE 49: FLYCATCHERS III

Tropical Kingbird *Tyrannus melancholicus*   L 22cm
Ar, **Bon**, **Cur** Pímpiri hel; **NL** Tropische koningstiran.
Largest of the yellow-bellied flycatchers on the islands and as such immediately recognisable. Head grey, back olive-grey, wings and tail brownish. *Whitish throat and underparts bright yellow*. Concealed orange crown patch. Rather heavy bill, tail slightly forked. Resident birds belong to ssp. *T. m. chloronotus* but darker birds of the nominate ssp. from central and southern South America may visit the islands. **Voice** Noisy with loud chirping *péé-prree-prree-prree*. **HH** Inhabits all kind of thorn scrub but especially near freshwater sites. Will perch on exposed branches or telephone wires from which it will chase after passing insects, always returning to its point of departure. **Status** Breeds on all three islands.

Grey Kingbird *Tyrannus dominicensis*   L 23cm
Ar, **Bon**, **Cur** Pímpiri gris; **NL** Grijze koningstiran.
Large all-grey flycatcher with immaculate white underparts, not yellow as in Tropical Kingbird; also larger head, heavier bill and sturdier build than that species. *The big head, heavy bill and a black stripe through the eye* distinguish it easily from Tropical Mockingbird with which it could be confused. In flight it *lacks the white tail-margins* of the latter species. Concealed red crown patch. Island population belong to nominate ssp. **Voice** Noisy with a jubilant, loud trill, *pee-cherrreee*. **HH** Usually occupies protruding branches, wires or any other prominent look-out post from which it will dive on insects passing by. Confiding. **Status** Breeds on all three islands.

Eastern Kingbird *Tyrannus tyrannus*   L 21cm
Ar Tirano cabez preto; **Bon** Tirano kabes pretu; **Cur** Not recorded; **NL** Koningstiran.
Looks like a black-and white Grey Kingbird. Upperparts blackish with *conspicuous white terminal band across tail*, a key characteristic of this species. Underparts white, concealed red crown patch. Bill shorter than in Grey Kingbird. **Voice** Usually silent on wintering grounds. On breeding grounds high staccato notes *dzee-dzee-dzee* or *kit-kit-kit*. **HH** On winter migration travels in flocks but on the islands only single stragglers have been reported. Prefers wooded areas but also visits farms and can be seen along the roadside. **Status** Rare visitor from North America. One record on Aruba and one on Bonaire.

PLATE 50: FLYCATCHERS IV

Fork-tailed Flycatcher *Tyrannus savana*   L 40cm
Ar Tirano rabo fòrki; **Bon**, **Cur** Pímpiri rab'i souchi; **NL** Vorkstaartvliegenvanger.
Elegant, slender bird with very long, **deeply forked black tail**. Black cap, nape and sides of head contrast with light grey upperparts. Underparts white, concealed crown patch yellow. Immature with brown cap and shorter tail. Adult may show shorter tail depending on stage of moult, but always shows clear tail fork, especially in flight. *T. s. monachus* from northern South America and nominate ssp. from southern South America both have been recorded – the first is more pure grey above than the latter which may appear rather dirty-grey. **Voice** Not very vocal. Soft twittering and a rapid *tic-tic-tic-tic*. **HH** Perches on fence-posts, dead branches or telephone wires, out in the open but preferably near fresh water. Often in small flocks. Very pugnacious, chases other flycatchers and even sandpipers and stilts. **Status** Regular visitor from North and South America.

Streaked Flycatcher *Myiodynastes maculatus*   L 22cm
Ar, **Cur** Not recorded; **Bon** Pímpiri strepiá; **NL** Gestreepte tiran.
Large, heavily streaked flycatcher. Bill very large with pinkish lower mandible. Upperparts brown streaked paler brown. Extensive rufous coloration in wings and in tail. **Streaked black, not brown, and with narrow rufous edges of wing coverts and tail feathers**. Unmistakable as it is the only flycatcher with such a streaked pattern observed on the islands. **Voice** A loud *squee-zik* and a penetrating *teep*. **HH** Often sits quietly in foliage, chasing after large insects like grasshoppers between the branches. **Status** Rare visitor from South America. One record of a single bird on Bonaire; subspecies not determined, but each of the three depicted races could occur on the islands.

PLATE 51: VIREOS

Philadelphia Vireo *Vireo philadelphicus* L 12cm
Ar, **Cur** Vireo Philadelphia; **NL** Philadelphiavireo.
Smallest vireo recorded on the islands and most easily confused with warblers, notably Tennessee Warbler. Above dull olive-green. *White eye-stripe without bordering black line. Black stripe through eye extends to base of bill.* Underparts *whitish to yellow*, especially on breast and including undertail-coverts. Tennessee Warbler has white undertail-coverts. Also bill thicker than in warblers. **Voice** Not often heard on wintering grounds. Song a repetitive *weej-weez-weezeech*, similar to Red-eyed Vireo but higher and more nasal. **HH** Same as other vireos, creeping through dense foliage looking for insects. **Status** Rare visitor from North America. Two records from Aruba and one from Curaçao.

Yellow-throated Vireo *Vireo flavifrons* L 14cm
Ar, **Bon** Not recorded; **Cur** Vireo pechu hel; **NL** Geelborstvireo.
Can be told from other two vireos by the *two white wingbars on the dusky grey wings and the bright yellow breast*. Upperparts yellowish-green with yellow 'spectacles' and belly white. Bill heavy for size of bird but shorter than in other vireos. Bill thicker than in similarly coloured warblers, which makes it easy to distinguish. **Voice** Usually a rapid, harsh *chep*. Occasionally fragments of song can be heard on wintering grounds, a melodious whistled *reeeooo-reeooee-reeeight*. **HH** Same habits as other vireos, moving deliberately through foliage in search of insects. **Status** Rare visitor from North America. One record on Curaçao.

Red-eyed Vireo *Vireo olivaceus* L 15cm
Ar Vireo wowo còrá; **Bon**, **Cur** Vireo wowo kòrá; **NL** Roodoogvireo.
Dull olive-green above with a contrasting grey cap. Facial pattern much more sharply defined than in Black-whiskered Vireo with a *black-bordered white eye-stripe*. Overall darker green than Black-whiskered with greener sides of head. *Red eye* conspicuous at close quarters. Immature with brown eye. No dark malar streak as in Black-whiskered Vireo. Bill remarkably thick for size of bird. **Voice** Not heard on winter quarters. Song a repetitive *hear me... see me... che-ve...* **HH** Very secretive, creeping through dense foliage in search of insects. Always on the move, often in small groups looking for insects. Also eats berries. **Status** Rare visitor from North America. Five records from both Bonaire and Curaçao and one from Aruba.

Black-whiskered Vireo *Vireo altiloquus* L 16cm
Ar Vireo patiya preto; **Bon**, **Cur** Vireo patia pretu; **NL** Baardvireo.
Dull olive-green above with greyish cap, less contrasting than in Red-eyed Vireo. Facial pattern less sharply defined than in latter species; white eye-stripe with only upper black border. Red-brown eye. *Black malar streak* ('whisker') definitive feature. Relatively heavy bill. Overall paler than Red-eyed Vireo. Residents belong to pale ssp. *V. a. bonairensis*. Migrants from Florida, Bahamas and Cuba belong to *V. a. barbatulus* which is *darker olive above, has more yellow and buff on the underside and a grey-buff eye-line*. Birds from Jamaica, Hispaniola, Puerto Rico belong to nominate ssp. which is *much greener, with darker upperparts and brownish sides of head and superciliary lines*. The resident ssp. of the Lesser Antilles, *A. a. barbadensis*, is *lighter green above and greyer below*. **Voice** A cheerful warble *tree-veerio*. **HH** Very secretive, more often heard than seen. Even when located by its song difficult to spot as it hides in dense foliage. Most often encountered in stands of fruit trees and in thorn bushes near fresh water. **Status** Breeding bird and visitor. Breeding has been recorded from all three islands. All ssp. have been recorded for the islands.

Yellow-throated Vireo

Philadelphia Vireo

adult fresh

adult worn

Red-eyed Vireo

vividor adult

chivi adult

olivaceus adult

juvenile

Black-whiskered Vireo

altiloquus adult

barbatulus adult

bonairensis adult

barbadensis adult

PLATE 52: MARTINS

Brown-chested Martin *Progne tapera* — L 18cm
Ar Swalchi pecho brùin; **Bon**, **Cur** Not recorded; **NL** Bruinborstzwaluw.
Upperparts light brown with darker wings and tail. Underparts white except for a brown chest band, not very well defined (northern South American nominate ssp.). When at rest may show *white undertail-coverts on either side of the tail* even when seen from above. This feature, along with size, distinguishes it from Bank Swallow and Southern Rough-winged Swallow. In ssp. of southern South America (*P. t. fusca*), which might occur as occasional migrant, the brown chest band extends to a vertical line down the centre of the chest. Only martin from the genus *Progne* which *lacks any shiny black plumage*. **Voice** Contact call a chirpy *chu-chu-chu*. Also a buzzy *d'jri-d'jri-d'jri*. **HH** Mostly seen over open terrain. Will forage quite low. Graceful flight. Perches on electricity wires, fence-posts or protruding branches. **Status** Rare visitor from South America. Four records from Aruba.

Purple Martin *Progne subis* — L 19cm
Ar Swalchi azul; **Bon**, **Cur** Souchi grandi blou; **NL** Purperzwaluw.
Very large swallow. Male black all over with a bluish sheen, only swallow on the islands with *completely dark belly*. In field however, almost indistinguishable from male Cuban Martin except the latter has a more deeply forked tail. Female more brownish with faint bluish sheen on crown and back. Grey, streaked breast and more whitish belly. Faint greyish neck band. Immature like female but with conspicuous dark streaks on belly and undertail. Female and immature may be confused with female and immature of Caribbean and Grey-breasted Martins. Belongs to nominate ssp. though other ssp. may occur, distinguished by size and amount of white in female. **Voice** A melodious descending whistled *cherr*. Alarm call a buzzing *geerrt*. **HH** Glides in circles for long periods, alternating with short bursts of flapping wings. Prefers habitat near fresh water. Mostly seen high in the air during autumn and spring passage. **Status** Rare visitor from North America. One record from Aruba, two from Bonaire and three from Curaçao.

Cuban Martin *Progne cryptoleuca* — L 19cm
Ar, **Bon** Not recorded; **Cur** Souchi grandi cubano; **NL** Cubaanse purperzwaluw.
Male like male of Purple and Caribbean Martins except for *white of underparts forming median line up to breast*. However, this white abdomen is *concealed* and can only be seen with the bird in hand. In flight, the more deeply forked tail distinguishes it from Purple Martin. Female and immature very difficult to distinguish from females and immature of other *Progne* species. White on belly more extensive in female Caribbean Martin, female Brown-chested Martin has white chin, female Purple Martin has pale collar and forecrown. **Voice** Similar to that of Caribbean and Purple Martin. Warbling song with a high *twick-twick*. **HH** Same flight pattern as Caribbean and Purple Martin. **Status** Rare visitor from Cuba. Collected on five occasions on Curaçao, but not reported from other islands. Probably often overlooked. Due to similarity of females and immature with other *Progne* species, only records of males have been accepted.

Caribbean Martin *Progne dominicensis* — L 19cm
Ar Swalchi grandi caribense; **Bon**, **Cur** Souchi grandi caribense; **NL** Caribische purperzwaluw.
Male looks like male Purple Martin but with *sharply demarcated white lower breast, belly and under tail-coverts*. Female much duller and very much like female of Purple Martin but no brown chest-band. Immature like female but unlike immature of Purple Martin *lacks dark streaks on breast, belly and undertail*. South American Grey-breasted Martin (*P. chalybea*, not recorded on the islands so far) resembles Purple and Caribbean Martin but male has grey throat, spreading to breast and merging with white belly. Female has no sharp demarcation between spotted brown breast and whitish belly. **Voice** A repertoire of tweets and peeps. Contact call *zoot*, alarm call *wheet* or *peek*. Song warbling. **HH** Similar to Purple Martin, flapping flight alternating with long glides in circles. Quite high in the air but may forage near ground too. **Status** Rare visitor from the West Indies. Reported during autumn and spring migration. Two records from Aruba, five from Bonaire and eight from Curaçao.

PLATE 53: SWALLOWS I

White-winged Swallow *Tachycineta albiventer* — L 13cm
Ar, **Bon** Not recorded; **Cur** Souchi barika blanku; **NL** Witbuikzwaluw.
Upperparts glossy bluish-green with large *white wing patches* and immaculate white underparts. White rump. Immature brownish, lacks white wing patches but has white rump. Tail black, slightly forked. **Voice** Call an agreeable *wreeeet*. Buzzing noises like *jee-reek*, song a trilled *zweed*. **HH** Found along freshwater ponds. Perches on rocks in the water or overhanging branches. Performs zig-zag flights over the water surface. **Status** Rare visitor from South America. One record on Curaçao.

Chilean Swallow *Tachycineta meyeni* — L 13cm
Ar, **Bon** Not recorded; **Cur** Souchi chileno; **NL** Chileense zwaluw.
Upperparts steel bluish-black. White rump and narrow white edges to innermost flight feathers. Underparts white with faint greyish breast band, more developed near sides. Tail slightly forked. Immature duller brown often with narrow white lines above lores. **Voice** Song a high-pitched gurgle with lower guttural sounds. **HH** Found near fresh water. **Status** Rare visitor from South America. Only one record from Curaçao of two birds, probably accidental as its northernmost distribution is southern Brazil, Paraguay and Bolivia.

Bank Swallow *Riparia riparia* — L 13cm
Ar Swalchi ribera; **Bon**, **Cur** Souchi ribera; **NL** Oeverzwaluw.
Upperparts uniformly coloured brown. Underparts white with *a contrasting brown band across breast*. Tail slightly forked. Immature more cinnamon above and buffy below. White extends behind ear. Always shows breast band. Brown-chested Martin much larger. Visiting birds belong to nominate ssp. **Voice** A chirpy *tschr* in flight or a sharper *schrrrt*. Song a broken twittering. **HH** Flight erratic and fluttery. **Status** Regular visitor from North America. The most common winter visitor on the islands, together with Barn Swallow. Most often seen during autumn migration, less often during spring. [Alt: Sand Martin]

Southern Rough-winged Swallow *Stelgidopteryx ruficollis* — L 14cm
Ar Swalchi di sùit; **Bon**, **Cur** Souchi di suit; **NL** Zuid-Amerikaanse ruwvleugelzwaluw.
Plain brown with somewhat darker wings and tail. *Conspicuous light brown to whitish rump in flight contrasting with rest of plumage*. Breast pale brown, gradually merging into whitish belly. Throat orange-brown. Undertail-coverts white. Lacks dark breast band of Bank Swallow with which it could be confused. **Voice** Twittering notes in flight and when perching. Call a buzzing *zzreet*. **HH** Flies in straight lines, going back and forth repeatedly, usually quite low above the ground. **Status** Rare visitor from South America. One record from Aruba, two from Bonaire and one from Curaçao.

PLATE 54: SWALLOWS II

Barn Swallow *Hirundo rustica*   L 16cm
Ar Swalchi; **Bon**, **Cur** Souchi; **NL** Boerenzwaluw.
Upperparts glossy bluish-black with *long, deeply forked tail*. Chestnut-brown chin and throat, underparts buff to white. *White spots on underside of tail distinctive* but can only be seen in flight and at close range. Females with white underparts and shorter tails. Immature duller with very little brown on head and short tails, white underparts. Visiting birds belong to the ssp. *H. r. erythrogaster*. **Voice** Usually silent on wintering grounds. Occasional *tweet* may be heard. **HH** Flight very graceful, swooping near ground or tree tops. May cruise tirelessly up and down. **Status** Regular visitor from North America. Very common on autumn passage when birds may arrive completely exhausted on the islands. Some years there is a great mortality among arriving birds.

Cliff Swallow *Petrochelidon pyrrhonota*   L 14cm
Ar Swalchi baranca; **Bon**, **Cur** Souchi baranka; **NL** Amerikaanse klifzwaluw.
Upperparts bluish-black with *contrasting buff-coloured rump*. A few white streaks on the back. Narrow buff neck collar. Head pattern with *creamy white forehead* and chestnut throat and sides of head, difficult to see in flight. Lower underparts white. *Tail square*, not forked as in Barn Swallow. **Voice** Contact call a soft *churr*, alarm call a rather plaintive *purr* and in flight *squeek*. Visting birds belong to nominate ssp. but the occurrence of *P. p. melanogaster* cannot be excluded. The latter is smaller with a cinnamon forehead and rump. **HH** Flies higher and glides more often than Barn Swallow. Often in mixed flocks with other swallows but never in high numbers. **Status** Regular visitor from North America. Mainly recorded during autumn migration.

Cave Swallow *Petrochelidon fulva*   L 13cm
Ar, **Bon** Not recorded; **Cur** Souchi kueba; **NL** Holenzwaluw.
Resembles Cliff Swallow but with *reddish-brown forehead*, not white. Throat more buff than chestnut. Rump chestnut-brown and *more profusely streaked white on back*. Tail slightly forked, not square as in Cliff Swallow. Island record relates to Mexican ssp. *P. f. pallida*. The occurrence of *P. f. cavicola* cannot be excluded. The latter is smaller and darker with deep blue crown and rufous cheeks, throat and rump. **Voice** Calls include *che,weet* or *cheweet*. **HH** Prefers open fields near fresh water. **Status** Rare visitor from Mexican Gulf area. Only one record known from Curaçao where it was collected from a mixed flock of swallows. Breeds in Mexico, New Mexico, Texas and Greater Antilles.

PLATE 55: WHEATEAR AND THRUSHES

Northern Wheatear *Oenanthe oenanthe* L 16cm
Ar Not recorded; **Bon**, **Cur** Chuchubi ala pretu; **NL** Tapuit.
In summer plumage light grey with black wings and black ear-coverts extending to the eyes. In winter plumage buff with brownish wings. However, always recognisable by **black inverted T on tail, contrasting sharply with white rump and white undertail**. In all plumages light underparts. Female like male in winter plumage. **Voice** Call a hard, tongue-clicking *chak-chak*. Also *chak-wheet* with second part more whistled. **HH** Typical ground bird, restless and whenever perched bobs incessantly, fanning its tail. Sudden runs alternating with abrupt stops. **Status** Rare visitor from North America. One record from Curaçao and one from Bonaire, both in northern winter.

Wood Thrush *Hylocichla mustelina* L 20cm
Ar, **Bon** Not recorded; **Cur** Chuchubi barika pintá; **NL** Amerikaanse boslijster.
Together with the three *Catharus* species, one of a group of brown thrushes with spotted underparts. Wood Thrush is distinguished from *Catharus* species by its **reddish-brown crown and neck and the numerous large round spots on its underparts**. It is also slightly larger and plumper than the other species. **Voice** Call a rapid *pip-pip-pip*. May give a toned-down version of song *po-po-po ee-o-lay*, the first notes soft, the latter ones rising and flute-like. **HH** Forages on the ground in dense undergrowth. Has habit of flicking its wing frequently. **Status** Rare visitor from North America. One record from Curaçao, probably exceptional as its wintering grounds are in Central America.

Swainson's Thrush *Catharus ustulatus* L 18cm
Ar Not recorded; **Bon**, **Cur** Chuchubi ringch'i wowo blanku; **NL** Dwerglijster.
Upperparts greyish-brown. Underparts dusky white with numerous spots on throat and extending to lower breast. **Buffy brown sides of head and buffy eye-ring** determining features to differentiate it from Grey-cheeked Thrush and Veery. However, immature may lack eye-ring. Overall warmer-coloured than Grey-cheeked Thrush. Records relate to ssp. *C. u. swainsoni* from boreal North America. **Voice** Call a short *whit*. Song often heard on wintering grounds, flute-like phrases, each ascending at the end. **HH** Travels in mixed flocks during spring and autumn migration. Not as terrestrial as the other species of brown thrushes. Forages in lower levels of trees up to the treetops. **Status** Rare visitor from North America. Two records from Curaçao and five from Bonaire.

Veery *Catharus fuscescens* L 18cm
Ar Not recorded; **Bon**, **Cur** Chuchubi brùin klá; **NL** Veery.
Upperparts uniformly reddish-brown, more rufescent than either Swainson's or Grey-cheeked Thrush. Underparts dusky white with **indistinct spots** on throat and breast. **Least spotted of the brown thrushes. Partial, dull eye-ring**. Overall impression paler than other brown thrushes. Records relate to *C. f. fuscescens* from E North America. **Voice** Call a low *phew*. Song, readily heard on wintering grounds, a liquid *vee-ur, vee-ur, vee-ur*, descending all the time. **HH** Forages on the ground and in dense undergrowth. In migration may join flocks of other thrushes. **Status** Rare visitor from North America. Recorded during spring and autumn migration. Known from three records on Curaçao and five from Bonaire.

Grey-cheeked Thrush *Catharus minimus* L 18cm
Ar Not recorded; **Bon**, **Cur** Chuchubi garganta pintá; **NL** Grijswangdwerglijster.
Upperparts olivaceous grey. Underparts dull white with numerous spots only on throat and breast. **Sides of head and neck dull grey and no conspicuous eye-ring** which sets it apart from Swainson's Thrush and Veery. However, grey cheeks may be difficult to see in the field. Duller-looking than Swainson's Thrush. Belongs to *C. m. minimus* from NE North America. **Voice** Call a high, nasal *quee-a*. Song, sometimes heard in late winter, *wee-wheeoo-titi-whee*, rising at the end. Song of Veery is descending. **HH** Forages on damp ground in dense underbrush. Solitary, though may migrate in mixed flocks with other thrushes. **Status** Rare visitor from North America. Recorded during autumn and spring thrush migration, often together with other *Catharus* species. Two records from Curaçao and six from Bonaire.

PLATE 56: WAXWING, THRASHERS AND MOCKINGBIRD

Cedar Waxwing *Bombycilla cedrorum* — L 18cm
Ar Parha di cedro; **Bon**, **Cur** Not recorded; **NL** Cederpestvogel.
The *black mask and pointed crest* are distinctive. Sleek appearance, vinaceous-brown with a yellow terminal tail band and red tips to secondaries. Immature has white face and lacks the black mask, is heavily streaked on back, breast and abdomen, lacks the red wing-tips but does show the yellow terminal tail band. **Voice** A very thin metallic *zeee*, sometimes quavering. **HH** Forages in fruit trees and berry-bearing shrubs. Mostly in flocks but on migration single birds occur. **Status** Rare visitor from North America. One record on Aruba.

Pearly-eyed Thrasher *Margarops fuscatus* — L 27cm
Ar Not recorded; **Bon**, **Cur** Chuchubi wowo blanku; **NL** Witoogspotlijster.
Brown mottled dusky above with whitish, heavily streaked and scaled underparts. *Milky white iris* very conspicuous. Tail with narrow white tip, bill rather long and yellowish or flesh-coloured. Overall impression is of a large, long-tailed thrush. Insular ssp. *M. f. bonairensis* restricted to Bonaire. **Voice** A pleasant, loud, thrush-like song but haltingly delivered. **HH** Distributed throughout the hilly region of northern and central Bonaire. In dry season concentrates near fruit trees. **Status** Breeding bird on Bonaire. Only once observed on Curaçao and no records from Aruba.

Brown Thrasher *Toxostoma rufum* — L 25cm
Ar, **Bon** Not recorded; **Cur** Chuchubi barika marká; **NL** Rosse spotlijster.
Upperparts reddish-brown including long tail. Two white and two black wingbars. Underparts heavily streaked with teardrop spots, not roundish spots as in brown thrushes. Streaking darkens lower down the belly. Iris pale yellow. Upper mandible black, lower one whitish. Legs brown. Immature has brown eyes. **Voice** Calls a sharp *chak* and a low whistled *peeuuuwi*. Song very varied, uttered in repeated phrases with pauses in between. **HH** Scurries through undergrowth, thorn bushes and in fruit trees. **Status** Rare visitor from North America. One record on Curaçao, probably exceptional as southernmost wintering grounds are on Cuba and the Bahamas.

Tropical Mockingbird *Mimus gilvus* — L 25cm
Ar, **Bon**, **Cur** Chuchubi; **NL** Tropische spotlijster.
Probably the most conspicuous bird of the islands. Light grey above with darker wings and tail. *White edges on tail and white terminal band* distinguish it from Grey Kingbird with which it might be confused. Dark line through eye bordered by white above. Underparts whitish. Immature spotted below and more brownish above. Insular ssp. *M. g. rostratus*, characterised by its elongated bill, is restricted to these islands and some small Venezuelan islands. **Voice** Very loud, jubilant thrush-like song, especially in early morning. May imitate song of other birds but fixed phrases *chee-chee-boo, chbee, chbee*. **HH** Observed in all kinds of habitat including near houses. In morning and late afternoon will sing on conspicuous spots like rooftops, sign posts, telephone wires etc. terrestrial in habits. Omnivorous, prefers fruit but will eat insects, small lizards and may even rob the nests of small birds. **Status** Breeds on all three islands.

PLATE 57: WARBLERS I

Blackburnian Warbler *Dendroica fusca* — L 13cm
Ar, **Bon**, **Cur** Chipe Blackburn; **NL** Sparrenzanger.
In breeding plumage male unmistakable with black and white plumage and bright orange and black face pattern. Female olive above and pale orange restricted to throat. In winter plumage paler but always with yellow throat which may show traces of orange, dusky earpatch bordered by yellow as in Black-throated Green Warbler but unlike latter **streaked above with two white stripes on back**. Also look for the yellow stripes on the head. **Voice** Call a full *chip*, a buzzing *zzee* in flight. Does not sing in winter quarters. **HH** Usually alone. Forages at higher levels in canopy. Cocks its tail and may droop its wings while foraging. **Status** Rare visitor from North America. Recorded once on Aruba and Curaçao and eight times on Bonaire.

Yellow-throated Warbler *Dendroica dominica* — L 13cm
Ar, **Cur** Not recorded; **Bon** Chipe garganta hel; **NL** Geelkeelzanger.
Grey warbler with striking **black-and white face pattern and yellow throat**. Underparts white with black streaking on the sides. Two white wingbars and white undertail feathers. Some white in uppertail feathers too. Female and immature similar but duller. **Supercilium is white in D. d. albilora** from Northern North America **and partly yellow in nominate** ssp. from south-eastern North America. **Voice** Song not heard on wintering grounds. Utters sharp *tsip* or a high *tsee* in flight. **HH** Usually found high in canopy where it creeps along the branches, much like Black-and-white Warbler. Feeds on all kinds of invertebrates. **Status** One observation on Bonaire. The bird had a yellow supercilium, meaning it belonged to the nominate ssp.

Golden-winged Warbler *Vermivora chrysoptera* — L 13cm
Ar, **Cur** Not recorded; **Bon** Chipe ala di oro; **NL** Geelvleugelzanger.
Grey warbler with strong black-and-white face pattern and yellow crown. Only warbler with combination of **yellow wing patch and black throat**. Female is duller with dusky mask and throat. From below shows conspicuous white tail corners in both sexes. Hybrids between Golden-winged and Blue-winged Warblers occur. One form, known as 'Lawrence's Warbler', has white on face and underparts replaced by yellow and white instead of yellow wing patches; upperparts are yellowish-green; another, 'Brewster's Warbler', looks like Blue-winged but has white underparts. Neither have so far been recorded from the islands. **Voice** Call in flight a short *zzip*. Song a four-note *zee-zaa-zaa-zaa* with first note higher. **HH** Usually travels in mixed flocks. Found in the canopy actively gleaning the leaves for insects. **Status** Rare visitor from North America. One record from Bonaire.

Blue-winged Warbler *Vermivora cyanoptera* — L 12cm
Ar Chipe ala blou; **Bon**, **Cur** Not recorded; **NL** Blauwvleugelzanger.
Face and underparts bright yellow. Upperparts greenish with bluish-grey wings. **Two conspicuous white wingbars**. **Small black line through the eye**. White spots on outer tail feathers, visible from below. Yellow Warbler is all yellow, has no white wingbars and no white in tail. See Golden-winged Warbler for description of hybrids with that species. **Voice** Song a buzzing *beeee-bzzz* as if inhaled and exhaled. Call a dry *zip*. **HH** Joins mixed flocks on wintering grounds, gleaning foliage for insects. Often flicks tail, showing the white spots on outer feathers. **Status** Rare visitor from North America. One record from Aruba.

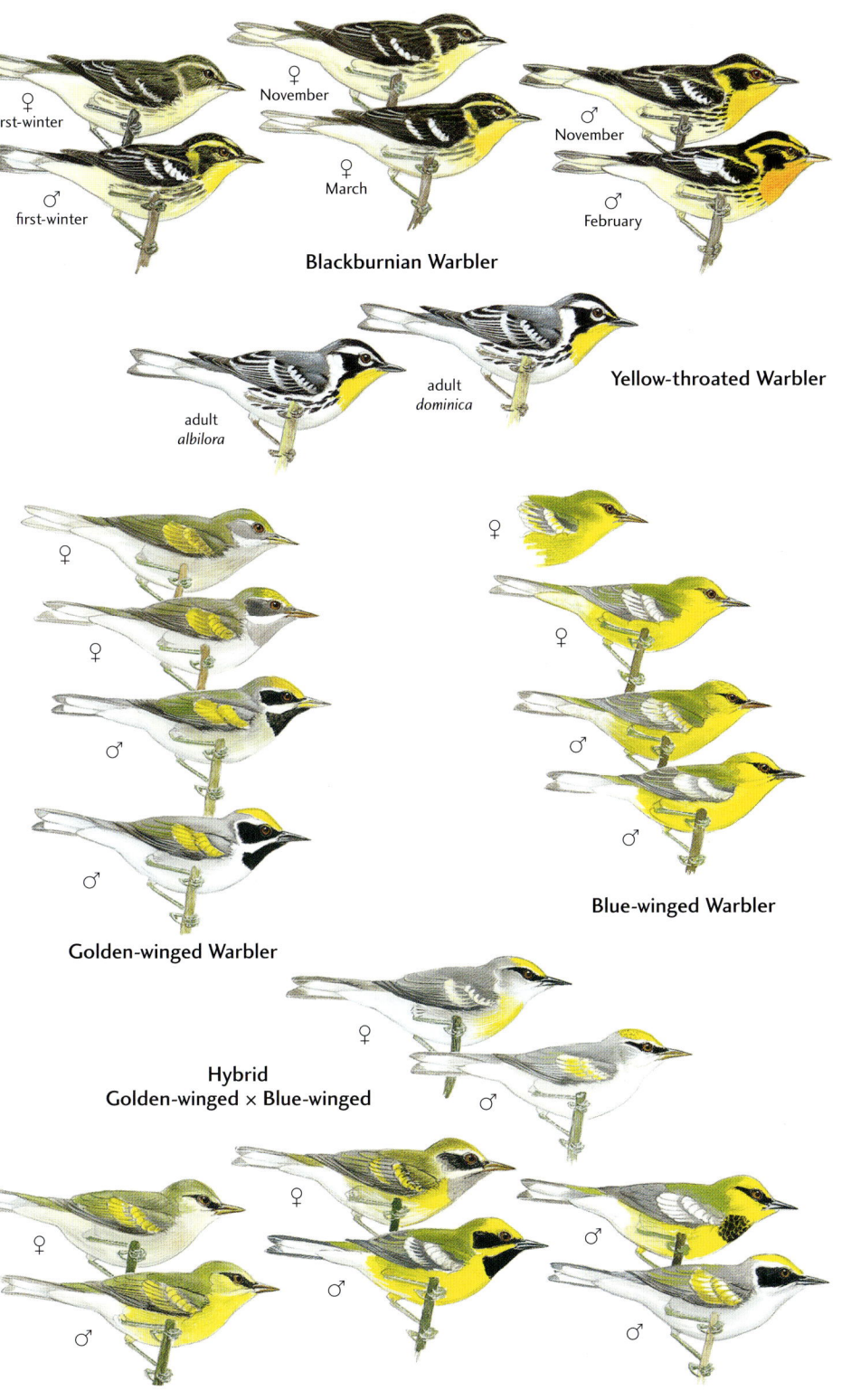

PLATE 58: WARBLERS II

Tennessee Warbler *Leiothlypis peregrina* L 12cm
Ar Not recorded; **Bon**, **Cur** Chipe Tennessee; **NL** Tennesseezanger.
Rather dull and nondescript warbler resembling Philadelphia Vireo except for *white undertail-coverts and very thin, sharply pointed bill*. Male greenish-olive with contrasting grey crown and grey face. White eye-stripe. Female and immature with more yellow, especially on underparts, and hint of a wingbar. Both immature and female have yellowish eye-stripe. Shows white undertail-coverts in all plumages. **Voice** In flight a sharp *tsit*. Song, on spring migration, a three-part *ticka-ticka-ticka, swit-swit-swit, chew-chew-chew*, each part with its own rhythm and pitch. **HH** Gleans foliage for insects but also visits flowering trees to take nectar from the blossoms. **Status** Rare visitor from North America. Four records from Bonaire and one from an oil tanker between Curaçao and Venezuela.

Northern Parula *Parula americana* L 11cm
Ar, **Bon**, **Cur** Chipe parula; **NL** Brilparulazanger.
Tiny, roundish warbler. Gives bluish impression, with yellow throat and two white wingbars. Underparts yellow; greenish patch on the back. Male with a *chestnut band across breast*, absent in female. Both sexes show *conspicuous broken white eye-ring*. Tropical Parula (*P. pitiayumi*) from South America lacks the breast band and shows no eye-ring; not yet recorded on islands. **Voice** Call a high, clear *tsip*. Song a buzzing ascending *zeeeeee-up*. **HH** Usually single. Found on the outer edge of foliage where it very busily checks the leaves and twigs for insects. **Status** Irregular visitor from North America. Reported from all three islands, but never in large numbers. Mainly encountered during winter months.

Black-throated Green Warbler *Dendroica virens* L 13cm
Ar, **Bon**, **Cur** Chipe lomba bèrdè; **NL** Gele zwartkeelzanger.
Male in breeding plumage immediately recognisable by *yellow face bordered by black chest and olive-green crown*. Female shows same pattern but with less extensive black on chest. Immature and adult in winter plumage may be easily confused with other warblers. *Greenish upperparts and facial pattern of dusky yellow earpatch bordered all around by bright yellow are points to look for*. **Voice** Call a sharp *zip*. Song, usually not heard in winter quarters, a slurred *tee-ew, tew, tew, tew wi*. **HH** Forages at somewhat low levels in vegetation, mainly for insects but eats fruits too. **Status** Rare visitor from North America. Two records from Aruba, four from Bonaire and one from Curaçao, all males showing more or less complete breeding plumage. Unconfirmed sightings of birds in winter plumage exist.

Yellow Warbler *Dendroica petechia* L 12cm
Ar Parha di misa.; **Bon** Chibichibi; **Cur** Para di misa; **NL** Gele zanger.
Bright yellow with pointed bill and dark, beady eyes. Male with *chestnut crown and chestnut streaks on breast and sides*. Female has greenish-yellow upperparts including crown, though some may show chestnut or partly chestnut crown. Faint to almost nonexistent streaking on sides of breast and flanks. Birds on the islands belong to the South Caribbean ssp. *D. p. rufopileata*. The North American ssp. *D. p. aestiva* may be expected here as a migrant; males lack chestnut crown but females indistinguishable in the field from local ssp. In the hand *D. p. aestiva* has longer wingtips and a longer bill. There are many other ssp., with males that have all-brown or all-yellow heads, but so far there are no records of these from the islands. **Voice** Call a soft, liquid *tree*. Song a warbling *tsee-tsee-tsee, tee-tee-tee,wee*, heard throughout the day. **HH** Very confiding. Can be found in all kinds of vegetation where it will look for insects, especially on the finest twigs. **Status** Breeds on all three islands.

Black-throated Blue Warbler *Dendroica caerulescens* L 13cm
Ar Chipe blou garganta preto; **Bon** Chipe blou garganta pretu; **Cur** Not recorded; **NL** Blauwe zwartkeelzanger.
Male unmistakable with blue upperparts, black sides and white belly. Female rather nondescript greenish-brown but *small white wing spot and dark ear-coverts with white supercilium* are determining features. Note also the absence of wingbars. Immature and female may lack white wing spot but show dark cheek. The birds recorded from Bonaire belonged to the nominate ssp. from N North America. **Voice** In flight a long *tseeet*. Call a short *chip* or *twik*. Song a lazy, ascending *zur,zur,zur,zree*. **HH** Forages for various food including insects, fruit and nectar. Often holds wings partially spread open. **Status** Rare visitor from North America. Three records from Aruba and five from Bonaire, all during autumn migration and all males. Females may easily be overlooked.

PLATE 59: WARBLERS III

Prairie Warbler *Dendroica discolor*   L 13cm
Ar, **Bon**, **Cur** Chipe pradera; **NL** Prairiezanger.
Yellow warbler with **black streaks on sides and black face pattern** in male. At close range note the chestnut spots on back. Female duller, face pattern paler and less distinct. Immature with less distinct streaking on sides. Like Palm Warbler bobs its tail incessantly. Face pattern distinguishes it from Yellow Warbler. **Voice** Call a sharp *tchuip* or a drier *chip*. In flight a high *seep*. Song a high, thin *zee, zee, zee*. **HH** Forages on all levels in vegetation. Seems to prefer flowering *Agave* plants, where it will take nectar. **Status** Rare visitor from North America. One record on Aruba of one bird which for six years returned annually to the same site for a few weeks in October. One record from Curaçao.

Prothonotary Warbler *Protonotaria citrea*   L 14cm
Ar, **Bon**, **Cur** Chipe lamoenchi; **NL** Citroenzanger.
Male bright orange-yellow head and underparts up to lower belly. Greenish back and grey-blue wings. Lower underparts and undertail-coverts white. White patches on tail feathers. Female same colour pattern but duller. No wingbars, no eye-stripes. Not easily confused as **white abdomen and white undertail-coverts** set it apart from any other yellow warbler. **Voice** Call a loud *chink*, in flight a clear *seeep*. **HH** Mostly solitary or in pairs. Forages on rotting tree trunks or fallen branches looking for insects. Also feeds on fruits, seeds and nectar. **Status** Regular visitor from North America. Recorded from all three islands though only three times on Curaçao. Never very numerous.

Chestnut-sided Warbler *Dendroica pensylvanica*   L 12cm
Ar Chipe flanco castaño; **Bon** Chipe banda koló castaño; **Cur** Not recorded; **NL** Roestflankzanger.
In breeding plumage easily identified by the chestnut line along breast and flanks, bordering the white underparts. Besides, both sexes show yellow crown. Upperparts green. In winter plumage facial pattern absent and only traces of chestnut lines remain. However, always shows **two yellow wingbars and white eye-ring**. Immature like winter adult but no traces of chestnut lines. May be confused with immature Bay-breasted Warbler but the latter has buff underparts and no eye-ring. **Voice** Call a simple *chip* or a harsher *zeet* in flight. Song, seldom heard on wintering grounds, similar to that of Yellow Warbler. **HH** Usually solitary. When moving through foliage the cocked tail is conspicuous. **Status** Rare visitor from North America. Three records from Aruba and ten from Bonaire.

Bay-breasted Warbler *Dendroica castanea*   L 13cm
Ar Chipe barica castaño; **Bon**, **Cur** Chipe barika kastaño; **NL** Kastanjezanger.
Male in breeding plumage has dark head, chestnut throat, breast and sides and conspicuous buff patch on neck. Female paler, head not uniformly dark, and buff sides. Immature and adult in winter plumage closely resemble Blackpoll Warbler but **buffier underparts** with **black feet**, not pale brown. *Traces of buff sides are most reliable characteristic*. Often in company of Blackpoll Warbler, allowing for comparison. **Voice** A high *tees, teesi, teesi*, quite similar to Cape May Warbler. Also resembles Black-and-white Warbler. **HH** Usually solitary and moves cautiously through vegetation looking for insects, fruits and nectar. **Status** Rare visitor from North America. One record from Aruba, two from Bonaire and two from Curaçao, all of which showed the buff stripes on the sides. Immature and birds lacking the buff sides probably often not identified correctly.

Prairie Warbler

Chestnut-sided Warbler

Prothonotary Warbler

Bay-breasted Warbler

PLATE 60: WARBLERS IV

Magnolia Warbler *Dendroica magnolia* L 12cm
Ar, **Bon**, **Cur** Chipe magnolia; **NL** Magnoliazanger.
In breeding plumage strongly patterned yellow and black warbler. White patches on wing, black mask and heavy black streaking on underparts. Yellow rump and in all plumages *shows a white band across tail*. Female has two narrower white wingbars. Winter plumage duller, like female but no black mask and *black spots rather than streaks* on underparts. Immature like female but no black streaking. Blackburnian Warbler lacks yellow rump and has different face pattern. **Voice** Call a soft *chip* or a more scolding *tshekk*. Song similar to Yellow Warbler but shorter phrases. **HH** Usually solitary but may mix with other warblers. Visits foliage at lower levels. **Status** Rare visitor from North America. Two records on Aruba, four from Bonaire and one from Curaçao, during autumn and spring migration.

Cape May Warbler *Dendroica tigrina* L 13cm
Ar Chipe Cabo May; **Bon**, **Cur** Chipe Kabo May; **NL** Tijgerzanger.
In breeding plumage male shows chestnut cheeks, two white wingbars which may look like one white patch, and heavily streaked yellow underparts. Female lacks chestnut cheeks and duller overall. In winter plumage male more like female, without chestnut cheeks, underparts may turn whitish with dark stripes. Both sexes recognisable by *yellow patch on side of neck and yellow rump* in all plumages. Immature female shows only traces of yellow, grey face extending to neck, grey streaking on underparts and two faint white wingbars. **Voice** A very high, thin *tsee-tsee*. Quite similar to Bay-breasted Warbler. **HH** Seems to prefer fruits over insects. Also takes nectar from flowers. **Status** Rare visitor from North America. Seven records from Aruba, three from Bonaire and one from Curaçao, all but one during spring migration when the birds are more recognisable.

Blackpoll Warbler *Dendroica striata* L 13cm
Ar Chipe pèchi preto; **Bon**, **Cur** Chipe pèchi pretu; **NL** Zwartkopzanger.
Male in breeding plumage distinguished by black cap and white cheeks. White underparts streaked with black. Could be confused with Black-and-white Warbler but the latter has a *striped crown and black cheeks*. Female is duller without black cap and grey rather than white cheeks. Winter plumage olive above and greenish below with fair amount of streaking. May be confused with Bay-breasted Warbler but distinguishing features are: *pale pinkish, not black, feet; white, not buff, undertail-coverts; greenish, not buff, underparts with more streaking*. **Voice** When feeding in groups a buzzing *zeet, zeet* resembling Bay-breasted Warbler. **HH** Always in loose groups, feeding on the ground and in low vegetation. **Status** Regular visitor from North America. It is the most common migrant warbler passing through the islands, particularly numerous during autumn migration.

Yellow-rumped Warbler *Dendroica coronata* L 13cm
Ar Chipe corona di oro; **Bon**, **Cur** Chipe korona di oro; **NL** Geelstuitzanger.
In breeding plumage male brightly coloured; blue-grey upperparts, yellow crown, rump and patch on side of chest. Black arch on chest. Female browner. In winter plumage both sexes brownish, no streaking on whitish undersides and no yellow crown. However, in all plumages *yellow rump and yellow patches on sides of chest* are determining features. Immature duller, greyish but still with yellowish rump. Immature Cape May Warbler more greenish rump, immature Palm Warbler browner and constantly bobs tail. The birds recorded from Curaçao belong to nominate ssp. with white throat and pale supercilium. The ssp. *D. c. auduboni*, more streaked with yellowish throat and no supercilium, has been recorded from Venezuela. **Voice** Call a loud distinctive *check* amid a variety of *chip, chup* and *chak* notes. **HH** Usually in groups or in mixed flocks. Visits all levels of vegetation and often looks for food on the ground. **Status** Rare visitor from North America. Two records from Aruba, five from Bonaire and two from Curaçao.

PLATE 61: WARBLERS V

Palm Warbler *Dendroica palmarum* L 13cm
Ar, Bon, Cur Chipe di palma; NL Palmzanger.
In breeding plumage brown above, yellow below with brownish streaks. Chestnut cap and yellow eye-stripe. Much browner and with **less streaking** than resident Yellow Warbler. Sexes similar. In winter plumage lacks the chestnut cap. **Yellow undertail-coverts** are conspicuous in all plumages. Unlike other warblers (except Prairie Warbler) constantly bobs of the tail when moving around. Records relate to the western nominate ssp. **Voice** A sharp but melodious *tchik* and in flight a high *tseet-tseet*. **HH** Feeds mainly on the ground on insects but also eats fruits and seeds. Will also visit flowering *Agave* plants. **Status** Rare visitor from North America. One record from Aruba, two from Bonaire and two from Curaçao.

Cerulean Warbler *Dendroica cerulea* L 11cm
Ar, Cur Not recorded; Bon Chipe blou garganta blanku; NL Azuurzanger.
Male clearly identifiable by bluish upperparts and white underparts with narrow black chest band. Female olive-green above with blue hue to crown and nape, whitish below. **Two white wingbars** distinguish it from Tennessee Warbler. Note the thick bill and relatively short tail. Imm female resembles autumn Blackpoll Warbler but much **more greenish and more distinct supercilium**. **Voice** Call a sharp, almost hissing *sship*, in flight a buzzing *zzzeee*. During spring migration may sing *zree, zree, zree, zreeet*. **HH** Forages at mid-levels to top of canopy. Difficult to spot as it gleans leaves for insects. **Status** Rare visitor from North America. Three records from Bonaire, all during autumn migration.

Worm-eating Warbler *Helmitheros vermivorum* L 13cm
Ar Not recorded; Bon, Cur Chipe kabes strepiá; NL Streepkopzanger.
Dull olive above with buff breast and sides, white belly. Crown with **four bold black stripes** which make it easily recognisable. **No wingbars, no streaking**. The cinnamon morph has light buff face and darker buff underparts. **Voice** Call a short *chip*, also a two-note *zeep-zeep*. **HH** More terrestrial than most warblers, looking for insects among dead leaves on the ground. **Status** Rare visitor from North America. Two records from Bonaire and one from Curaçao.

Black-and-white Warbler *Mniotilta varia* L 13cm
Ar Chipe trepador; Bon, Cur Chipe kabes abou; NL Bonte zanger.
Only really black-and-white patterned warbler occurring on the islands. Male with black throat and cheeks. Might be confused with Blackpoll Warbler in summer plumage but the latter has **black cap and white cheeks**. Female duller and more whitish below. Maybe could be confused with autumn Blackpoll Warbler but the latter is **greenish and has no striped crown**. **Voice** Call a sharp *tik*, which may extend to a rapid series *tiktiktiktik* in alarm. May sing during winter migration, a thin *weesee, weesee, weesee*. **HH** Prefers montane forest but on migration may be found in any habitat. May creep along trunks and branches looking for insects. **Status** Irregular visitor from North America. Various observations from the different islands but never very numerous and almost always single birds.

American Redstart *Setophaga ruticilla* L 13cm
Ar Rabo còrá americana; Bon, Cur Rabu kòrá; NL Amerikaanse roodstaart.
Male black with **bright orange patches** on wings and tail. Female olive-green and with **yellow** instead of orange patches. Immature like female but immature male may show some orange. Unique tail-pattern makes it unmistakable. **Voice** Not heard singing on wintering grounds. Call a thin, clear *chip*, in flight an ascending *tweet*. **HH** Very active, fluttering through the trees while spreading wings and tail repeatedly. **Status** Regular visitor from North America. Very common warbler on the islands during winter but presence dependent on amount of water.

PLATE 62: WARBLERS VI

Kentucky Warbler *Oporornis formosus* L 13cm
Ar, Bon, Cur Chipe di Kentucky; NL Kentuckyzanger.
Strong head pattern is determining feature. Above olive-green without any spots, stripes or wingbars. Underparts yellow. Black forehead with black extending to sides of neck, forming typical '*sideburns*'. Yellow line around the eye forms '*spectacles*'. In female black less extensive and in immature black may be absent. Female and immature may be confused with Common Yellowthroat but latter *lacks yellow 'spectacles'*. Canada Warbler is *grey above and shows dark necklace*. **Voice** Call a sharp, low *chok*, in series when alarmed. In flight a buzzing *zzeep*. **HH** Quite terrestrial in habits, turning over dead leaves to look for insects. Tail cocked and often flicked. **Status** Rare visitor from North America. One record from Aruba, seven from Bonaire and one from Curaçao, all but one in October.

Common Yellowthroat *Geothlypis trichas* L 12cm
Ar Mascarita comun; Bon, Cur Maskarita komun; NL Gewone maskerzanger.
Male easily recognisable by black mask bordered above with white edge. Brownish-olive above, yellow throat and chest with brownish flanks and *white abdomen*. Female lacks black mask and can be identified by combination of *yellow chest, white belly and brownish flanks*. May show a faint eye-ring. No yellow 'spectacles' as in Kentucky Warbler. **Voice** Call a husky *tchip* and a longer *jieerk*. **HH** Encountered in marshy vegetation on the shores of freshwater ponds. Wren-like in behaviour, almost always hidden in dense undergrowth. **Status** Irregular visitor from North America. Most often recorded on Aruba with only one sighting for Curaçao and one for Bonaire.

Hooded Warbler *Wilsonia citrina* L 14cm
Ar Chipe velo preto; Bon Chipe belo pretu; Cur Not recorded; NL Monnikszanger.
Male with black hood and yellow face mask. Upperparts olive-green, underparts yellow. Female and immature lack strong features but in some females the yellow face is outlined sharply. In all sexes look for *white edges of outer tail feathers*. Remarkably large eyes. Female Prothonotary Warbler distinguished from female Hooded Warbler by *grey wings and no hint of hood*. **Voice** Call a metallic *chink* or a longer *chippety-chup* in encounters with competitors. Song may be heard, a whistled ascending *weeta-weeta-weete-o*. **HH** Found in dense shrub at the edges of freshwater pools and in fruit plantations. Usually keeps well hidden but may sally forth like a bright yellow flycatcher. **Status** Irregular visitor from North America. Several records from Aruba and Bonaire but none from Curaçao.

Canada Warbler *Wilsonia canadensis* L 13cm
Ar, Bon, Cur Chipe canades; NL Canadese zanger.
Male uniformly grey above, yellow below. Black 'sideburns' and typical *black necklace*. White underbelly and undertail-coverts. Yellow stripe on forecrown and around the eyes form spectacles. Female and immature usually have traces of necklace. When absent, as in some imm., look for the *yellow spectacles*. Also grey upperparts with yellow underparts and lack of white in wings and tail conclusive. **Voice** Call a sharp *chip*. Song, ocasionally heard during migration, a staccato *chip, chippety-twee, dwitchetee*. **HH** Solitary or in mixed flocks in dense undergrowth. Often droops wings and cocks tail. May fan tail. **Status** Rare visitor from North America. One record from Bonaire.

Mourning Warbler *Oporornis philadelphia* L 13cm
Ar, Cur Chipe di luto; Bon Not recorded; NL Grijskopzanger.
Male with grey head gradually changing to *black patch on chest*. Olive-green above and underparts yellow. Female duller with brownish-grey hood. Immature has suggestion of a hood and broken white eye-ring. Female usually has *no eye-ring*, in contrast to Connecticut Warbler, but much variation – some females show almost complete eye-ring. Female has *paler throat and breast* than Connecticut Warbler. Looks more plump than Connecticut Warbler with more upright posture. **Voice** A sharp *chak* and a high *swit* in flight. Song, heard during spring migration, *chirree-chirree-chori-chori*, final notes lower. **HH** Solitary, skulks through undergrowth looking for insects. Usually near water. **Status** Rare visitor from North America. Two records from Aruba and two from Curaçao, all during autumn migration.

PLATE 63: WARBLERS VII AND BANANAQUIT

Connecticut Warbler *Oporornis agilis*   L 14cm
Ar, **Bon**, **Cur** Chipe di Connecticut; **NL** Connecticutzanger.
Male with grey hood extending to chest, olive-green above and yellow below. Female and immature duller, with brownish-grey hood. Undertail-coverts yellow and reach almost to the tip of the tail. All plumages show an **unbroken eye-ring** which sets it apart from Mourning Warbler. **Voice** A sharp metallic *plink*, in flight a buzzy *zee*. **HH** Mostly solitary, walks with tail and head bobbing. Terrestrial in habits, looking for insects under dead leaves. Rather tame and confiding, **running rather than hopping** among low brushes and grass patches. Relatively long legs. **Status** Regular visitor from North America but never very numerous.

Louisiana Waterthrush *Parkesia motacilla*   L 14cm
Ar, **Bon**, **Cur** Chipe di sur; **NL** Louisianawaterlijster.
Similar to Northern Waterthrush, differences being **white supercilium instead of creamy, white unstriped chin, and white to creamy underparts with lighter stripe markings**. Bill also somewhat heavier but difference is subtle. **Voice** A slightly metallic *tseek*, louder than in Northern Waterthrush, uttered in series when alarmed. **HH** Same habitat and same behaviour as Northern Waterthrush though it seems to be slower in its movements. **Status** Rare visitor from North America. Three records from Aruba, two from Curaçao and five from Bonaire.

Northern Waterthrush *Parkesia noveboracensis*   L 14cm
Ar, **Bon**, **Cur** Chipe di norte; **NL** Noordelijke waterlijster.
Upperparts brown, supercilium **creamy-yellowish** which sets it apart from Louisiana Waterthrush. Chin and underparts **creamy and heavily striped dark**. Long pink legs. A form exists in which supercilium and underparts are more whitish, hence more difficult to distinguish from Louisiana Waterthrush. **Voice** A clear metallic *tsseek*, sometimes in series when alarmed. **HH** Terrestrial in habits, found on shores of freshwater ponds but also on any damp, shady soil. Looks for insects in horizontal posture with bobbing tail. **Status** Regular visitor from North America. Observed on all three islands during migration periods.

Ovenbird *Seiurus aurocapilla*   L 15cm
Ar Chipe di fòrno; **Bon**, **Cur** Chipe di fòrnu; **NL** Ovenvogel.
Looks like a small thrush. Brown above, white below and heavily streaked. Conspicuous **orange crown stripe bordered by black stripes**, only visible at close range. This, and **white eye-ring** set it apart from waterthrushes which it may resemble in habits. Pink legs. Visiting birds are of nominate ssp. from E North America though one individual showed characters of the western ssp. *S. a. cinereus*. **Voice** Loud characteristic call *teach'er, teach'er*, not often heard. Utters sharp *tchik* notes. **HH** Terrestrial in habits, scurrying through dense undergrowth particularly on moist soil, looking for insects under dead leaves. **Status** Regular visitor from North America. Various observations from all three islands but never numerous. Due to its secretive habits probably often overlooked.

Bananaquit *Coereba flaveola*   L 12cm
Ar Barica hel; **Bon** Bachi pretu; **Cur** Barika hel; **NL** Suikerdiefje.
Probably most popular bird of the islands. Upperparts black including sides of head, bright yellow underparts. Conspicuous **white eye-line and red edge of mouth**. Ssp. from Bonaire (*C. f. bonairensis*) differs from ssp. from Aruba and Curaçao (*C. f. uropygialis*) by having a much larger white central area on the throat, always clearly visible. In *C. f. uropygialis* the white on the throat is only visible when the bird lifts its head. **Voice** Song a chirrupy ill-defined, slurred whistle without any clear notes, compared to retreating waves on a shelly beach. **HH** Occurs in any habitat. Will visit flowering plants in small parties with much chasing among the group. Flowers with deep calyces will be pierced at the bottom to reach the nectar. Will readily visit tables with uncovered sugar pots to take the sugar. **Status** Breeds on all three islands.

PLATE 64: TANAGERS AND HONEYCREEPER

Scarlet Tanager *Piranga olivacea* — L 17cm
Ar Tanagre còrá; Bon, Cur Tanagre kòrá; NL Zwartvleugeltangare.
Male in summer plumage bright red with **black wings and tail**. In winter olive-green above, yellow-green below with black wings and tail. In female wings and tail dusky. Immature like female; immature male may show patched red and green plumage when moulting to adult plumage. Some immature Scarlet Tanagers may show two yellowish wingbars. Female Summer Tanager has *lighter wings*, Western Tanager shows *wingbars*. **Voice** Call a hoarse *chip-burr*. Song not heard on wintering grounds. **HH** Usually solitary. Shows same behaviour as Summer Tanager. **Status** Regular visitor from North America, but never very numerous. Most observations during spring migration. Only a few records from Aruba.

Summer Tanager *Piranga ruber* — L 17cm
Ar Not recorded; Bon, Cur Tanagre ala pretu; NL Zomertangare
Male rosy red all over with yellowish bill. Maintains this colour during winter, in contrast to Scarlet Tanager. Female olive-yellowish above with yellowish-green underparts. May be confused with Scarlet Tanager but the latter has *darker wings*. Western Tanager has *wingbars*. Immature like female; immature male may show red and green patched plumage when changing to adult plumage. **Voice** Call a staccato *pick-a-cup, pi-tuck*. Song not heard on wintering grounds. **HH** Moves unhurriedly through foliage. Sallies forth after flying insects but also gleans twigs. **Status** Rare visitor from North America. Two records from Bonaire and two from Curaçao.

Western Tanager *Piranga ludoviciana* — L 18cm
Ar, Cur Not recorded; Bon Tanagre barika hel; NL Louisianatangare.
Male in summer plumage bright yellow with black wings and tail and red head. In winter plumage red on head disappears. Female olive above, dull yellow below. Both sexes always show *one yellow and one white wingbar*. Immature like female but head and rump paler giving *a saddle-backed look* which distinguishes it from the few immature Scarlet Tanagers with two wingbars. **Voice** Mostly silent during migration. In flight a soft whistled *howee*. **HH** Usually solitary but may form flocks on migration. Moves through foliage looking for insects. **Status** Rare visitor from North America. One record from Bonaire.

Red-legged Honeycreeper *Cyanerpes cyaneus* — L 13cm
Ar Not recorded; Bon, Cur Barika blou; NL Blauwe suikervogel.
Unmistakable. Male in breeding plumage bright blue with azure cap and black mask. Upper back and wings black. Long curved bill and bright red legs. Outside breeding plumage blue changes to green. Female and immature green with grey-green striped underparts. In both sexes underwing-coverts are yellow, visible in flight. Immature like female. **Voice** Constantly utters weak *tsip* notes. **HH** Restless little bird found in treetops where it will look for nectar or small insects. Also eats berries and punctures larger fruit. **Status** Rare visitor from South America. Two records from Bonaire, of immature male and immature female moulting into adult plumage, and two records from Curaçao.

PLATE 65: SWALLOW TANAGER, WEAVERS AND SPARROW

Swallow Tanager *Tersina viridis* — L 15cm
Ar Not recorded; **Bon**, **Cur** Tanagra souchi; **NL** Zwaluwtangare.
No other bird with these colours on the islands. Male bright turquoise with black face mask. Centre of lower breast and belly white, blue flanks barred with black. Female green with yellowish and green barred underparts. **Voice** Call a buzzy *tzeet*. Song a squeaky twitter. **HH** Gregarious, always in small groups of several males and females. Eats small fruits but also chases after insects. **Status** Rare visitor from South America. One record from Bonaire and one from Curaçao.

Baya Weaver *Ploceus philippinus* — L 15cm
Ar, **Bon** Not recorded; **Cur** Flègtudó skur; **NL** Bayawever.
Male in breeding plumage with bright yellow crown and breast. Black cheeks and lores, black bill. Upperparts streaked with yellow, underparts yellowish-buff. Female with brown upperparts streaked with buff, underparts greyish-buff. Supercilium buff. Non-breeding male resembles female in plumage. Might be confused with female House Sparrow but thick conical bill sets it apart. **Voice** Song a continuous *chit-chit-chit* ending in *chee-ee-ee*. Several males may join in. **HH** Builds nests dangling from the end of branches, always several together in breeding colony. **Status** Introduced species. Originally from east Africa and south-east Asia. A small breeding colony now established on Curaçao.

Village Weaver *Ploceus cucullatus* — L 14cm
Ar, **Bon** Not recorded; **Cur** Flègtudó hel; **NL** Grote Textorwever.
Male bright yellow with black face and throat. Dusky flight feathers and black wing coverts with yellow edges. Scapulars black. Non-breeding male has yellow head and olive crown; more greyish above and whitish below than in breeding plumage. Female brownish with dusky streaks. Underparts dirty yellowish. Supercilium yellowish. In all plumages black-and-yellow wings and thick conical bill make confusion with other species almost impossible. **Voice** A harsh chatter. Rasping song ending in a wheeze, *chit-chit-tttt-t-t-t-shirrzzzrrreeh*. **HH** Makes intricately woven nests hanging from branches. Nests in colonies. Confiding. **Status** Introduced species. Originally from East Africa. Small breeding colony now established on Curaçao.

House Sparrow *Passer domesticus* — L 14cm
Ar Parha di Joonchi; **Bon** Not recorded; **Cur** Para di Jonchi; **NL** Huismus.
Male grey with brown neck and wings. Grey rump. ***White sides of head and black throat***. Underparts grey. Female greyish-brown all over and without the black throat. Immature like female but greyish-white below. May be confused with Rufous-collared Sparrow but the latter has **dark head stripes and a slight crest**. **Voice** Song a monotonous *chirrup-chirrup*. **HH** Always occurs in small colonies. Tends to stay close to human habitation with nests made under the roofs of houses. However, also builds nests in palms. **Status** Breeding bird. Originally introduced from the Netherlands, now a common bird on Curaçao and Aruba.

PLATE 66: GROSBEAKS AND BUNTINGS

Rose-breasted Grosbeak *Pheucticus ludovicianus* — L 19cm
Ar Pico grandi pecho ros; **Bon**, **Cur** Pik grandi pechu ros; **NL** Roodborstkardinaal.
Rather plump bird with very thick bill. Male in summer plumage with **large rose-red triangle on breast**. Black upperparts with white wing patches, white wingbars and white rump, very conspicuous when in flight. In winter plumage streaked brown with buff eye-line and striped crown. Almost always shows traces of rose colour, especially on underside of wing. Female like male in winter plumage but no rose colour. Underside of wings *yellowish*. Bill **uniformly horn-coloured**, unlike Black-headed Grosbeak. Conspicuous white wingbars. **Voice** Call a metallic *click*. No song on wintering grounds. **HH** Forages high in canopy. However, on the islands mostly found in residential areas with large gardens. **Status** Irregular visitor from North America. Unpredictable occurrence but recorded on all three islands.

Black-headed Grosbeak *Pheucticus melanocephalus* — L 19cm
Ar, **Bon** Not recorded; **Cur** Pik grandi kabes pretu; **NL** Zwartkopkardinaal.
Like Rose-breasted Grosbeak with black head and black wings, and same white pattern. Back black streaked with orange-brown. Rump, breast, neck collar and sides *orange-yellow*. Female much like female Rose-breasted Grosbeak but breast *more ochre* and underside *less heavily streaked or unstreaked*; *bill clearly bicoloured*, darker above, lighter below. Underside of wing more clearly yellow. Immature like female. **Voice** A high and sharp *pik*. In flight a soft *wheez*. **HH** The only bird observed was found in manchineel trees lining a beach. **Status** Rare visitor from North America. Only observation was one adult male on Curaçao.

Blue Grosbeak *Passerina caerulea* — L 19cm
Ar, **Cur** Not recorded; **Bon** Pik grandi blou; **NL** Blauwe bisschop.
Male deep violet-blue, striped on back and wings with two chestnut wingbars. In winter plumage the feathers have rusty tips, giving the bird a mottled appearance. Female warm brown, lighter below, with **two buff wingbars**. Female may be confused with female Indigo Bunting but the latter is smaller and has no wingbars. Female Shiny Cowbird is more greyish-brown, lacks wingbars and has a much thinner bill. **Voice** A sharp *chink*. Song not heard on wintering grounds. **HH** Prefers dense undergrowth. Often flicks and fans its tail. **Status** Rare visitor from North America. One record from Bonaire, in residential garden.

Indigo Bunting *Passerina cyanea* — L 14cm
Ar Parha ìndigo; **Bon**, **Cur** Para ìndigo; **NL** Indigogors.
Male in summer plumage bright cyan-blue all over. Female plain brown without any distinguishing features. Male turns brown in winter plumage but usually retains traces of blue, giving a chequered appearance. Conical bill black above and whitish below. Female smaller than female Blue Grosbeak with **no wingbars**. Almost certainly often overlooked as female easily confused with female grassquits. **Voice** Call a sharp, thin *spit*. Song may be heard on spring migration, *seet-seet*, *chew-chew*, very lively. **HH** Can be found on harvested fields of millet during spring migration, feeding on the seeds which have fallen on the ground. **Status** Irregular visitor from North America. Of irregular occurrence on Bonaire and Curaçao and only one record from Aruba.

Dickcissel *Spiza americana* — L 15cm
Ar Arozero; **Bon** Not recorded; **Cur** Para di aña dashi gris; **NL** Dickcissel.
Resembles House Sparrow but has **grey head with yellowish eye-stripe** and **small black patch on breast**. Lower breast yellow and shoulders chestnut. In winter plumage male loses black patch on breast. Female like female House Sparrow but with yellowish eye-stripe and **chestnut shoulders**. Both sexes usually show some yellow, also in winter. **Voice** When occurring in flocks a constant twittering can be heard. Also when roosting the twittering goes on. **HH** Normally occurs in large flocks, feeding on the ground on grass seeds. However, on the islands all records are of singles or small groups. **Status** Irregular visitor from North America. Recorded mainly during autumn migration on Aruba and Curaçao. No records from Bonaire. May easily be overlooked.

PLATE 67: GRASSQUITS, SAFFRON FINCH AND SPARROWS

Blue-black Grassquit *Volatinia jacarina* — L 10cm
Ar Not recorded; **Bon**, **Cur** Mòfi bachi blou; **NL** Jacarinagors.
Male glossy blue-black all over. Small white patch at bend of wing and white underwing-coverts, visible in flight. Male has mottled appearance in fresh plumage as the feathers have brown fringes. These wear off quickly, leaving the bird all blue. Female brown, more buffy-brown below with **streaked breast and flanks**. May be confused with female Black-faced Grassquit but latter shows no streaking. **Voice** Song, given at the top of a display jump, is an explosive *bis'zeeer*, quite unlike Black-faced Grassquit. **HH** Same habitat as Black-faced Grassquit. Inspects stems of grasses and weeds for insects. Also eats the seeds. **Status** Rare visitor from South America. One record from Bonaire and one from Curaçao.

Black-faced Grassquit *Tiaris bicolor* — L 10cm
Ar, **Bon**, **Cur** Mòfi; **NL** Maskergrondvink.
Small finch-like bird with conical bill. Male looks completely black but under close observation shows dark olive upperparts and greyish flanks. Female and immature greyish-brown. Bill black and flesh-coloured legs. Local birds assigned to endemic ssp. *T. b. sharpei*, smaller and paler than other ssp. **Voice** Song very pleasant twitter *tsee-tsee-tsee tseetseetsee... peee*, the last very high and loud note delivered with bill wide open. Song delivered from conspicuous post or during short display flight with quivering wings. **HH** Most numerous in dry acacia and cactus shrub with abundant weeds, the seeds of which it will eat. **Status** Breeds on all three islands.

Saffron Finch *Sicalis flaveola* — L 14cm
Ar Parha hel; **Bon** Kanari; **Cur** Saffraanvink; **NL** Gewone saffraanvink.
Male bright yellow with orange crown. Upperparts more olive. Female somewhat duller. Immature with grey head and belly, yellow band across the chest, streaked grey above and below. Might be confused with Yellow Warbler but typical heavy finch bill makes identification easy. Island birds belong to nominate ssp. from northern South America. **Voice** Song a rather monotonous *cheep-cheep chit chit*. Call a dry *tsit*. **HH** Occurs in small family flocks. Feeds on seeds on the ground. **Status** Breeding bird. One of the more recent arrivals on the islands, establishing itself in the 1970s. Breeds on Bonaire and Curaçao. Formerly not uncommon on Aruba but apparently it has disappeared there.

Grasshopper Sparrow *Ammodramus savannarum* — L 11cm
Ar Not recorded; **Bon**, **Cur** Mòfi di sabana; **NL** Sprinkhaangors.
Very secretive small bird, difficult to observe. Back striped chestnut and black, dark cap with buff median stripe. **Head looks flattened**. Underparts white but with unstreaked buff breast. Pointed tail feathers. A small ochre spot before eye may extend to above eye. Bend of wing yellowish. Immature shows some dark streaking below. Local birds belong to the endemic ssp. *A. s. caribaeus*, characterised by short bill, small size and pale plumage. **Voice** Song an insect-like buzzing, very high and metallic *chirp... pee-tsee-zee-zee-zee* delivered with wide-open bill. **HH** Very local in distribution, preferring open scrub with patches of grass and weeds. **Status** Breeds on Bonaire and Curaçao. No records from Aruba.

Rufous-collared Sparrow *Zonotrichia capensis* — L 15cm
Ar, **Bon**, **Cur** Chonchorogai; **NL** Roodkraaggors.
Upperparts rufous streaked with black, grey head with black stripes. **Chestnut neck collar and black patch on side of breast**. Underparts whitish. Always shows small crest, giving the head a squared-off appearance. Immature has brown head with white supercilium, underparts streaked black. Belongs to palest and smallest ssp. *Z. c. insularis*. **Voice** Song very pleasant *tsee-tsee-trrreee*, ending in trill. Only bird on the islands to sing at night. **HH** Wide range of habitats as long as shrubs and small trees are present. **Status** Breeds on all three islands but much less numerous on Bonaire, where the bird was introduced from Curaçao.

White-throated Sparrow *Zonotrichia albicollis* — L 17cm
Ar Chonchorogai garganta blanco; **Bon**, **Cur** Not recorded; **NL** Witkeelgors.
Upperparts streaked chestnut and black with grey breast and black and white (or brown and ochre) head stripes. **Very broad yellowish or white supercilium. White throat patch conspicuous**. Narrow black line separating throat-patch from malar patch. Might be confused with Rufous-collared Sparrow but the latter has chestnut neck band and black patch on side of breast. **Voice** A soft *tsseeet* and a harder *chink*. **HH** On wintering grounds found in gardens. Prefers woody, shrubby areas. **Status** Rare visitor from North America. One record on Aruba, probably exceptional as its normal wintering grounds are the southern United States and northern Mexico.

PLATE 68: STARLING AND ICTERIDS I

Common Starling *Sturnus vulgaris*   L 20cm
Ar, **Bon** Chuchubi Oropeo; **Cur** Not recorded; **NL** Spreeuw.
Gives an all-black impression at first but sunlight reveals purple and green iridescence. Long, thin, pointed yellow bill. Long legs. Winter plumage much duller with numerous white spots; bill turns blackish. Immature duller, brownish without the iridescent shimmer on the feathers. **Voice** An endless chattering in roosting places when large flocks settle down. Call a buzzy *churr*. **HH** Gregarious but only a few stragglers have reached the islands. In behaviour as bold as Caribbean Grackle. Mostly terrestrial in habits, probing for worms and other small animals. **Status** Rare visitor from Greater Antilles or North America. Originally from Europe but introduced into United States and also on Jamaica and Cuba. Two records from Aruba and one from Bonaire. [Alt: European Starling]

Bobolink *Dolichonyx oryzivorus*   L 18cm
Ar Parha di aña; **Bon**, **Cur** Para di aña; **NL** Bobolink.
Male in breeding plumage black with white scapulars, lower back and rump. Yellow neck patch. Winter male like female, very sparrow-like, upperparts buff streaked black with **dark stripes on head**. Underparts yellowish-buff with some streaking. Immature may show more yellow on underparts. Tail in all plumages shows individual feather tips at the end, giving it a spiky appearance. Males attain breeding plumage by spring migration. **Voice** In summer quarters travels in flocks, calling to each other in loud *chep-chep* notes. **HH** Terrestrial in habits. Forages for seeds on the ground and in grass and weeds. Usually in large flocks but on migration may appear in small groups of just a few birds. **Status** Regular visitor from North America. Can be observed during autumn and spring migration. Numbers may vary greatly between years.

Yellow-hooded Blackbird *Agelaius icterocephalus*   L 18cm
Ar Not recorded; **Bon**, **Cur** Trupial pretu kabes hel; **NL** Geelkaptroepiaal.
Male black with bright yellow head and breast. Black spot connecting eye and black bill. Female olive striped with grey, with yellowish line above eye and **yellowish head and breast**, separating it from more brownish-olive underparts, recalling male's colour pattern but in much more muted colours. **Voice** Call a dry *check*. Song a squeaky *took,took-weeze* the last note drawn out. **HH** Usually moves around in flocks. Found on flat land with lots of grass or low shrubs. Feeds on invertebrates and seeds. **Status** Rare visitor from South America. One record from Curaçao and two from Bonaire, all males.

Eastern Meadowlark *Sturnella magna*   L 24cm
Ar, **Cur** Not recorded; **Bon** Chuchubi dashi pretu; **NL** Witkaakweidespreeuw.
Upperparts mottled brown, head striped white and brown. Yellow below, lighter on sides with black streaks. **V-shaped black patch on breast**. Long bill and legs but relatively short wings and tail. White outer tail feathers. Immature more buff coloured with the V-shaped patch broken up into spots. **Voice** A slurred whistled *cheewa-seea, chewa-chorra*. **HH** Terrestrial in habits. When moving around often spreads tail showing white outer tail feathers. **Status** Rare visitor from South America. One record from Bonaire.

PLATE 69: ICTERIDS II

Carib Grackle *Quiscalus lugubris* — L 26cm
Ar Zenata caribeña; **Bon, Cur** Zenata karibeño; **NL** Caribische troepiaal.
Male shining black all over with conspicuous *white iris*. Back and sides irridescent violet-black, wings a shimmering greenish-black. Tail held in V-shape, which in flight gives the impression of the tail being held in vertical position. Female dark brown above, lighter below. Breeding birds belong to nominate ssp. from northern Venezuela. **Voice** Very noisy, uttering loud squeaking noises like rusty hinges. **HH** Very bold, almost arrogant in behaviour. Forages mainly on ground, common to urban areas. Prefers to hide in date palms and forages around mangroves, so is very common where both are close to each other. **Status** Breeds on all three islands.

Great-tailed Grackle *Quiscalus mexicanus* — L 33–43cm
Ar, Bon Not recorded; **Cur** Zenata rabu largu; **NL** Langstaarttroepiaal.
Male considerably larger than female. Male steely blue-black with conspicuous *white iris*. Very long tail held in V-shape. Female dark brown above and paler below. Vague buff supercilium. Immature has brown eyes. Much larger than Carib Grackle. **Voice** Utters a very loud rising whistle but also makes harsher sounds. **HH** Strutting behaviour but not as urban as Carib Grackle. On the islands sticks to mangroves. Scavenges for anything edible. **Status** Uncertain. For years a small group never surpassing five birds resided in mangroves near the DOK on Curaçao. However, when the mangroves died off the birds disappeared and no recent sightings have been recorded. They probably originally came from South America.

Greater Antillean Grackle *Quiscalus niger* — L 30cm
Ar Zenata antiano; **Bon, Cur** Not recorded; **NL** Antilliaanse troepiaal.
Male very much like male Carib Grackle, slightly larger and with a stronger bill. Iris is light yellow but may appear white. Female is smaller and duller than male but black, not brown. Immature has light brown iris. **Voice** Makes harsh and rasping sounds *chak-chak* intermixed with higher *whee-see-see* notes. **HH** Usually in flocks. Prefers open areas but readily visits urban parks or gardens. **Status** Rare visitor from Greater Antilles. One record from Aruba, after passing of hurricane.

Shiny Cowbird *Molothrus bonariensis* — L 19cm
Ar Parha vakero lustroso; **Bon, Cur** Para vakero lustroso; **NL** Glanskoevogel.
Male glossy steel-blue black, *dark eye*. Female dull brown, upperparts a shade darker than underparts, also dark-eyed. Might be confused with Carib Grackle but the latter has *white eyes* and is much more slender in overall shape with longer bill and V-shaped tail. Also, the behaviour is quite different, though male Shiny Cowbirds may parade with puffed-up chests in front of females. Breeding birds belong to *M. b. venezuelensis* from northern Venezuela. **Voice** Song a pleasant melodious whistle *purr-purr-purr-ptseeeee*. **HH** Wide-ranging in habitat, mostly preferring scrub vegetation with open spaces. Brood parasite, known to lay eggs in nests of Yellow Oriole. **Status** Breeds on all three islands.

Red-breasted Blackbird *Sturnella militaris* — L 19cm
Ar Chuchubi pecho còrá; **Bon, Cur** Not recorded; **NL** Zwartkopsoldatenspreeuw.
Male all black with bright red throat and breast. Female has heavily streaked brown and buff upperparts, underparts buff with *rose tinge to chest*. Head with buff eye-stripe and median crown stripe. Resembles female and autumn male Bobolink and Dickcissel but those species have more yellowish underparts. Immature lacks rose, has thick dark brown streaks on belly. **Voice** Call a harsh *pleek* and a dry rattle. Song consists of a few weak notes followed by a long trill, *e-sec-er-leeeezz*. **HH** Usually seen in flocks. Terrestrial in habits, looking on the ground for insects and seeds. **Status** Rare visitor from South America. Only one record from Aruba.

PLATE 70: ICTERIDS III

Venezuelan Troupial *Icterus icterus*   L 25cm
Ar, **Bon**, **Cur** Trupial; **NL** Oranje troepiaal.
Very brightly coloured orange and black bird. Black of head and back **separated by orange band**. **Black wings with large white patch**. Skin around eye blue, iris pale yellowish. Immature much paler and more yellow. Unmistakable; Baltimore Oriole is smaller and has no orange neck band and no large white patch on the wings. The birds on the islands belong to the ssp. *I. i. ridgwayi*. **Voice** A melodious yodling *troo-pee-oo* delivered from some high point like a rooftop, sign post or candelabra cactus. **HH** Prefers lush vegetation where it feeds on fruits, readily visits gardens. Also eats insects and even will rob nests of small birds. **Status** Breeds on all three islands.

Baltimore Oriole *Icterus galbula*   L 19cm
Ar, **Bon** Trupial di Baltimore; **Cur** Not recorded; **NL** Baltimoretroepiaal.
Male bright orange and black with black of the head and throat **extending to neck and back**. Black wings with white wingbar and white edgings. Female and immature olive-brown above and orange-yellow below. Immature male may show the beginnings of the black hood. Two white wingbars. Might be confused with Venezuelan Troupial but much smaller and the **white on the wings less extensive**, not forming a large patch. **Voice** Call a low, whistled *hew-li*. Song a rich melodious whistle. **HH** Usually single. Inspects bundles of dead leaves for insects. Visits flowering trees. **Status** Irregular visitor from North America. Recorded on Aruba and Bonaire during autumn and spring migration.

Orchard Oriole *Icterus spurius*   L 17cm
Ar, **Bon** Not recorded; **Cur** Trupial shouru; **NL** Tuintroepiaal.
Male all-black except for dark orange-chestnut rump and underparts. One white wingbar on black wing. Female yellowish-grey above with two white wingbars. Underparts more greenish-yellow. First-year male like female but with a black throat. Strong bill sets it apart from warblers with which it could otherwise be confused due to small size. Female and immature Baltimore Oriole are more orange-yellow. **Voice** Call loud slurred *wheer*. Song a rich warble with piping whistles and more guttural notes. **HH** Forages at all levels. Visits flowering trees. At nightfall hides in thick bushes. **Status** Rare visitor from North America. One record from Curaçao.

Yellow Oriole *Icterus nigrogularis*   L 21cm
Ar Gonzalito; **Bon**, **Cur** Trupial kachó; **NL** Gele troepiaal.
Mainly bright yellow with black around eye, **black throat**, tail and wings with **one white wingbar**. Iris black. Immature lacks black throat, upperparts more golden-green. Wing and tail olive-brown. Immature lacks black throat patch and upperparts more golden-green. Birds from the islands belong to the ssp. *I. n. curasoensis*, paler yellow and with more white in wing than other ssp. **Voice** Most frequently heard call is a scratchy metallic *chet-chet-chet*, song flute-like *teee-tuu*, not very loud. **HH** Builds long cylindrical nests hanging from the tips of branches, often using the same nest site year after year, but building a new nest each time. More often found in drier areas with thorn shrub and cacti than Venezuelan Troupial. Feeds on large insects, fruits and nectar. **Status** Breeds on all three islands.

Oriole Blackbird *Gymnomystax mexicanus*   L 28cm
Ar Zenata mexicano; **Bon**, **Cur** Not recorded; **NL** Wielewaaltroepiaal.
Very large, bright yellow bird with black back, wings and tail. Black area around the eye and **black malar mark**. Yellow patch on wing. Might be confused with Yellow Oriole but large size, **no white in wings, heavy bill and no black throat** set it apart. Immature paler without black mask and yellow wing patch but shows a black cap. **Voice** Call a high screech, like rusty hinges. Unmusical song, a buzzy *shweek, shweek, shweek*. **HH** Terrestrial in habits, visiting open grassy spaces to look for insects, seeds and fruits. **Status** Rare visitor from South America. Recorded once on Aruba.

APPENDIX

Introduced parrots and parakeets

Over the years several escaped parrots have established viable populations, particularly on Curaçao, but also on Aruba. These species are treated in the main text on Plates 39 and 40. They tend to remain mostly in residential areas with many gardens.

Occasional escapees

The species below occasionally escape from captivity, but are not established:

Egyptian Goose *Alopochen aegyptiaca*
Ar, **Bon**, **Cur** Gans di Nilo; **NL** Nijlgans.

Orinoco Goose *Neochen jubata*
Ar, **Bon**, **Cur** Gans di Orinoko; **NL** Orinocogans.

Scarlet Macaw *Ara macao*
Ar, **Bon**, **Cur** Wakamaya Venezolana; **NL** Rode ara.

Blue-and-yellow Macaw *Ara ararauna*
Ar, **Bon**, **Cur** Wakamaya blou-hel; **NL** Blauw-gele ara.

Cockatiel *Nymphicus hollandicus*
Ar, **Bon**, **Cur** Prikichi falcón; **NL** Valkparkiet.

Hill Myna *Gracula religiosa*
Ar, **Bon**, **Cur** Beo; **NL** Grote beo.

Zebra Finch *Taeniopygia guttata*
Ar Parha zebra; **Bon**, **Cur** Para zebra; **NL** Zebravink.

CHECKLIST OF THE BIRDS OF ARUBA, CURAÇAO AND BONAIRE

The taxonomy and nomenclature used in this checklist mainly follows those of the American Ornithologists' Union (AOU) and its South American Checklist Committee (SACC).

Globally Threatened Species (GTS) Species considered to be globally threatened by BirdLife International are assigned one of the following codes, based on IUCN Red List criteria:
EN (Endangered), **VU** (Vulnerable) or **NT** (Near Threatened).

		Aruba	Curaçao	Bonaire	GTS
Ducks and Geese – Anatidae					
Fulvous Whistling-Duck	*Dendrocygna bicolor*	●		●	
White-faced Whistling-Duck	*Dendrocygna viduata*	●	●	●	
Black-bellied Whistling-Duck	*Dendrocygna autumnalis*	●	●	●	
Greater White-fronted Goose	*Anser albifrons*	●			
Comb Duck	*Sarkidiornis melanotos*	●	●	●	
American Wigeon	*Anas americana*	●	●	●	
Mallard	*Anas platyrhynchos*			●	
Green-winged Teal	*Anas crecca*	●	●		
Northern Pintail	*Anas acuta*	●		●	
White-cheeked Pintail	*Anas bahamensis*	●	●	●	
Blue-winged Teal	*Anas discors*	●	●	●	
Cinnamon Teal	*Anas cyanoptera*	●			
Northern Shoveler	*Anas clypeata*	●		●	
Ring-necked Duck	*Aythya collaris*	●	●	●	
Lesser Scaup	*Aythya affinis*	●	●	●	
Bufflehead	*Bucephala albeola*			●	
Masked Duck	*Nomonyx dominicus*		●	●	
New World Quails – Odontophoridae					
Crested Bobwhite	*Colinus cristatus*	●	●		
Grebes – Podicipedidae					
Least Grebe	*Tachybaptus dominicus*	●	●	●	
Pied-billed Grebe	*Podilymbus podiceps*	●	●	●	
Flamingos – Phoenicopteridae					
American Flamingo	*Phoenicopterus ruber*	●	●	●	
Petrels and Shearwaters – Procellariidae					
Black-capped Petrel	*Pterodroma hasitata*	●	●	●	EN
Bulwer's Petrel	*Bulweria bulwerii*		●		
Great Shearwater	*Puffinus gravis*			●	
Audubon's Shearwater	*Puffinus lherminieri*		●	●	
Storm-Petrels – Hydrobatidae					
Wilson's Storm-Petrel	*Oceanites oceanicus*	●	●	●	
Leach's Storm-Petrel	*Oceanodroma leucorhoa*		●	●	

		Aruba	Curaçao	Bonaire	GTS
Tropicbirds – Phaethontidae					
Red-billed Tropicbird	*Phaethon aethereus*		●	●	
White-tailed Tropicbird	*Phaethon lepturus*		●	●	
Storks – Ciconiidae					
Wood Stork	*Mycteria americana*	●			
Frigatebirds – Fregatidae					
Magnificent Frigatebird	*Fregata magnificens*	●	●	●	
Great Frigatebird	*Fregata minor*	●			
Boobies – Sulidae					
Masked Booby	*Sula dactylatra*	●	●	●	
Red-footed Booby	*Sula sula*	●	●	●	
Brown Booby	*Sula leucogaster*	●	●	●	
Cormorants – Phalacrocoracidae					
Neotropic Cormorant	*Phalacrocorax brasilianus*	●			
Double-crested Cormorant	*Phalacrocorax auritus*			●	
Pelicans – Pelecanidae					
Brown Pelican	*Pelecanus occidentalis*	●	●	●	
Herons, Bitterns and Egrets – Ardeidae					
Boat-billed Heron	*Cochlearius cochlearius*			●	
Pinnated Bittern	*Botaurus pinnatus*	●			
Least Bittern	*Ixobrychus exilis*		●		
Black-crowned Night-Heron	*Nycticorax nycticorax*	●	●		
Yellow-crowned Night-Heron	*Nyctanassa violacea*	●	●	●	
Green Heron	*Butorides virescens*	●	●		
Striated Heron	*Butorides striata*		●	●	
Cattle Egret	*Bubulcus ibis*	●	●	●	
Great Blue Heron	*Ardea herodias*	●	●	●	
Great Egret	*Ardea alba*	●	●	●	
Whistling Heron	*Syrigma sibilatrix*			●	
Tricolored Heron	*Egretta tricolor*	●	●	●	
Reddish Egret	*Egretta rufescens*	●	●	●	NT
Little Egret	*Egretta garzetta*	●			
Snowy Egret	*Egretta thula*	●	●	●	
Little Blue Heron	*Egretta caerulea*	●	●	●	
Ibises and Spoonbills – Threskiornithidae					
White Ibis	*Eudocimus albus*	●			
Scarlet Ibis	*Eudocimus ruber*	●		●	
Glossy Ibis	*Plegadis falcinellus*	●		●	
White-faced Ibis	*Plegadis chihi*	●			
Roseate Spoonbill	*Platalea ajaja*	●	●	●	
New World Vultures – Cathartidae					
Turkey Vulture	*Cathartes aura*	●			
Osprey – Pandionidae					
Osprey	*Pandion haliaetus*	●	●	●	
Hawks and Kites – Accipitridae					
White-tailed Kite	*Elanus leucurus*	●			

		Aruba	Curaçao	Bonaire	GTS
Swallow-tailed Kite	*Elanoides forficatus*	●		●	
Northern Harrier	*Circus cyaneus*		●		
White-tailed Hawk	*Geranoaetus albicaudatus*	●	●	●	
Caracaras and Falcons – Falconidae					
Crested Caracara	*Caracara cheriway*	●	●	●	
Yellow-headed Caracara	*Milvago chimachima*		●	●	
American Kestrel	*Falco sparverius*	●	●	●	
Merlin	*Falco columbarius*	●	●	●	
Peregrine Falcon	*Falco peregrinus*	●	●	●	
Limpkin – Aramidae					
Limpkin	*Aramus guarauna*	●			
Rails and Gallinules – Rallidae					
Sora	*Porzana carolina*	●	●	●	
Common Gallinule	*Gallinula galeata*	●	●	●	
Purple Gallinule	*Porphyrio martinicus*	●	●	●	
Caribbean Coot	*Fulica caribaea*	●	●	●	NT
American Coot	*Fulica americana*	●	●	●	
Sungrebe – Heliornithidae					
Sungrebe	*Heliornis fulica*			●	
Lapwings and Plovers – Charadriidae					
Southern Lapwing	*Vanellus chilensis*	●	●	●	
American Golden-Plover	*Pluvialis dominica*	●	●	●	
Black-bellied Plover	*Pluvialis squatarola*	●	●	●	
Semipalmated Plover	*Charadrius semipalmatus*	●	●	●	
Piping Plover	*Charadrius melodus*			●	NT
Wilson's Plover	*Charadrius wilsonia*	●	●	●	
Killdeer	*Charadrius vociferus*	●	●	●	
Snowy Plover	*Charadrius nivosus*	●	●	●	
Collared Plover	*Charadrius collaris*	●	●	●	
Oystercatchers – Haematopodidae					
American Oystercatcher	*Haematopus palliatus*	●	●	●	
Stilts and Avocets – Recurvirostridae					
Black-necked Stilt	*Himantopus mexicanus*	●	●	●	
American Avocet	*Recurvirostra americana*			●	
Thick-knees – Burhinidae					
Double-striped Thick-knee	*Burhinus bistriatus*		●		
Sandpipers and Allies – Scolopacidae					
Wilson's Snipe	*Gallinago delicata*	●	●	●	
Short-billed Dowitcher	*Limnodromus griseus*	●	●	●	
Long-billed Dowitcher	*Limnodromus scolopaceus*	●	●	●	
Hudsonian Godwit	*Limosa haemastica*	●	●		
Whimbrel	*Numenius phaeopus*	●	●	●	
Upland Sandpiper	*Bartramia longicauda*	●	●	●	
Spotted Sandpiper	*Actitis macularius*	●	●	●	
Greater Yellowlegs	*Tringa melanoleuca*	●	●	●	
Lesser Yellowlegs	*Tringa flavipes*	●	●	●	

		Aruba	Curaçao	Bonaire	GTS
Solitary Sandpiper	*Tringa solitaria*	●	●	●	
Willet	*Tringa semipalmata*	●	●	●	
Ruddy Turnstone	*Arenaria interpres*	●	●	●	
Red Knot	*Calidris canutus*	●	●	●	
Sanderling	*Calidris alba*	●	●	●	
Semipalmated Sandpiper	*Calidris pusilla*	●	●	●	
Western Sandpiper	*Calidris mauri*	●	●	●	
Least Sandpiper	*Calidris minutilla*	●	●	●	
White-rumped Sandpiper	*Calidris fuscicollis*	●	●	●	
Baird's Sandpiper	*Calidris bairdii*	●	●	●	
Pectoral Sandpiper	*Calidris melanotos*	●	●	●	
Dunlin	*Calidris alpina*		●	●	
Stilt Sandpiper	*Calidris himantopus*	●	●	●	
Buff-breasted Sandpiper	*Tryngites subruficollis*	●	●	●	NT
Wilson's Phalarope	*Phalaropus tricolor*		●	●	
Red-necked Phalarope	*Phalaropus lobatus*		●	●	
Red Phalarope	*Phalaropus fulicarius*			●	
Jacanas – Jacanidae					
Wattled Jacana	*Jacana jacana*		●	●	
Skuas and Jaegers – Stercorariidae					
Great Skua	*Stercorarius skua*		●		
Pomarine Jaeger	*Stercorarius pomarinus*	●			
Parasitic Jaeger	*Stercorarius parasiticus*	●	●	●	
Long-tailed Jaeger	*Stercorarius longicaudus*	●	●	●	
Gulls and Terns – Laridae					
Black-headed Gull	*Chroicocephalus ridibundus*			●	
Bonaparte's Gull	*Chroicocephalus philadelphia*		●		
Laughing Gull	*Leucophaeus atricilla*	●	●	●	
Franklin's Gull	*Leucophaeus pipixcan*	●			
Ring-billed Gull	*Larus delawarensis*	●		●	
Lesser Black-backed Gull	*Larus fuscus*	●			
Herring Gull	*Larus argentatus*	●		●	
Great Black-backed Gull	*Larus marinus*	●		●	
Brown Noddy	*Anous stolidus*	●	●	●	
Black Noddy	*Anous minutus*	●		●	
Sooty Tern	*Onychoprion fuscatus*	●	●	●	
Bridled Tern	*Onychoprion anaethetus*	●	●	●	
Least Tern	*Sternula antillarum*	●	●	●	
Large-billed Tern	*Phaetusa simplex*	●			
Gull-billed Tern	*Gelochelidon nilotica*	●	●	●	
Caspian Tern	*Hydroprogne caspia*	●	●	●	
Black Tern	*Chlidonias niger*	●	●	●	
Common Tern	*Sterna hirundo*	●	●	●	
Roseate Tern	*Sterna dougallii*	●	●	●	
Cabot's Tern	*Thalasseus acuflavida*	●	●	●	
Royal Tern	*Thalasseus maximus*	●	●	●	

		Aruba	Curaçao	Bonaire	GTS
Skimmers – Rynchopidae					
Black Skimmer	*Rynchops niger*	●	●	●	
Pigeons and Doves – Columbidae					
Common Ground-Dove	*Columbina passerina*	●	●	●	
Ruddy Ground-Dove	*Columbina talpacoti*			●	
Rock Pigeon	*Columba livia*	●	●	●	
Scaly-naped Pigeon	*Patagioenas squamosa*	●	●	●	
Bare-eyed Pigeon	*Patagioenas corensis*	●	●	●	
Eared Dove	*Zenaida auriculata*	●	●	●	
White-tipped Dove	*Leptotila verreauxi*	●	●	●	
Parrots, Parakeets and Macaws – Psittacidae					
Rose-ringed Parakeet	*Psittacula krameri*		●		
Chestnut-fronted Macaw	*Ara severus*	●	●		
Blue-crowned Parakeet	*Aratinga acuticaudata*		●		
Scarlet-fronted Parakeet	*Aratinga wagleri*		●		
Brown-throated Parakeet	*Aratinga pertinax*	●	●	●	
Green-rumped Parrotlet	*Forpus passerinus*	●	●		
Red-lored Parrot	*Amazona autumnalis*		●		
Yellow-shouldered Parrot	*Amazona barbadensis*	●	●	●	VU
Yellow-crowned Parrot	*Amazona ochrocephala*		●		
Orange-winged Parrot	*Amazona amazonica*		●		
Cuckoos – Cuculidae					
Yellow-billed Cuckoo	*Coccyzus americanus*	●	●	●	
Mangrove Cuckoo	*Coccyzus minor*	●	●	●	
Grey-capped Cuckoo	*Coccyzus lansbergi*			●	
Greater Ani	*Crotophaga major*	●	●		
Groove-billed Ani	*Crotophaga sulcirostris*	●	●		
Barn Owls – Tytonidae					
Barn Owl	*Tyto alba*		●	●	
Owls – Strigidae					
Burrowing Owl	*Athene cunicularia*	●			
Oilbird – Steatornithidae					
Oilbird	*Steatornis caripensis*	●			
Nightjars and Nighthawks – Caprimulgidae					
Lesser Nighthawk	*Chordeiles acutipennis*		●	●	
Common Nighthawk	*Chordeiles minor*	●	●	●	
Antillean Nighthawk	*Chordeiles gundlachii*		●		
Chuck-will's-widow	*Antrostomus carolinensis*	●	●		
White-tailed Nightjar	*Caprimulgus cayennensis*	●	●		
Swifts – Apodidae					
Black Swift	*Cypseloides niger*		●		
Chimney Swift	*Chaetura pelagica*	●	●	●	NT
Hummingbirds – Trochilidae					
White-necked Jacobin	*Florisuga mellivora*	●	●		
Rufous-breasted Hermit	*Glaucis hirsutus*		●		
Ruby-topaz Hummingbird	*Chrysolampis mosquitus*	●	●	●	

		Aruba	Curaçao	Bonaire	GTS
Blue-tailed Emerald	*Chlorostilbon mellisugus*	●	●	●	
Kingfishers – Alcedinidae					
Ringed Kingfisher	*Megaceryle torquata*	●	●		
Belted Kingfisher	*Megaceryle alcyon*	●	●	●	
Amazon Kingfisher	*Chloroceryle amazona*	●			
Woodpeckers – Picidae					
Yellow-bellied Sapsucker	*Sphyrapicus varius*	●	●	●	
Tyrant Flycatchers – Tyrannidae					
Caribbean Elaenia	*Elaenia martinica*	●	●	●	
Small-billed Elaenia	*Elaenia parvirostris*	●	●		
Lesser Elaenia	*Elaenia chiriquensis*		●	●	
Northern Scrub-Flycatcher	*Sublegatus arenarum*	●	●	●	
Olive-sided Flycatcher	*Contopus cooperi*			●	NT
Eastern Wood-Pewee	*Contopus virens*	●			
Vermilion Flycatcher	*Pyrocephalus rubinus*	●			
Cattle Tyrant	*Machetornis rixosa*	●			
Streaked Flycatcher	*Myiodynastes maculatus*			●	
Tropical Kingbird	*Tyrannus melancholicus*	●	●	●	
Fork-tailed Flycatcher	*Tyrannus savana*	●	●	●	
Eastern Kingbird	*Tyrannus tyrannus*	●		●	
Grey Kingbird	*Tyrannus dominicensis*	●	●	●	
Brown-crested Flycatcher	*Myiarchus tyrannulus*	●	●	●	
Vireos – Vireonidae					
Yellow-throated Vireo	*Vireo flavifrons*		●		
Philadelphia Vireo	*Vireo philadelphicus*	●	●		
Red-eyed Vireo	*Vireo olivaceus*	●		●	
Black-whiskered Vireo	*Vireo altiloquus*	●	●	●	
Swallows and Martins – Hirundinidae					
Southern Rough-winged Swallow	*Stelgidopteryx ruficollis*	●	●	●	
Brown-chested Martin	*Progne tapera*	●			
Purple Martin	*Progne subis*	●	●	●	
Caribbean Martin	*Progne dominicensis*	●	●	●	
Cuban Martin	*Progne cryptoleuca*			●	
White-winged Swallow	*Tachycineta albiventer*			●	
Chilean Swallow	*Tachycineta meyeni*			●	
Bank Swallow	*Riparia riparia*	●	●	●	
Barn Swallow	*Hirundo rustica*	●	●	●	
Cliff Swallow	*Petrochelidon pyrrhonota*	●	●	●	
Cave Swallow	*Petrochelidon fulva*			●	
Waxwings – Bombycillidae					
Cedar Waxwing	*Bombycilla cedrorum*	●			
Chats and Old World Flycatchers – Muscicapidae					
Northern Wheatear	*Oenanthe oenanthe*		●	●	
Thrushes – Turdidae					
Veery	*Catharus fuscescens*		●	●	
Grey-cheeked Thrush	*Catharus minimus*		●	●	

		Aruba	Curaçao	Bonaire	GTS
Swainson's Thrush	*Catharus ustulatus*		●	●	
Wood Thrush	*Hylocichla mustelina*		●		
Mockingbirds and Thrashers – Mimidae					
Tropical Mockingbird	*Mimus gilvus*	●	●	●	
Brown Thrasher	*Toxostoma rufum*		●		
Pearly-eyed Thrasher	*Margarops fuscatus*		●	●	
Starlings – Sturnidae					
Common Starling	*Sturnus vulgaris*	●		●	
Tanagers – Thraupidae					
Swallow Tanager	*Tersina viridis*		●	●	
Red-legged Honeycreeper	*Cyanerpes cyaneus*		●	●	
Bananaquit and Grassquits – Incertae sedis					
Bananaquit	*Coereba flaveola*	●	●	●	
Black-faced Grassquit	*Tiaris bicolor*	●	●	●	
Seedeaters and Allies – Emberizidae					
Rufous-collared Sparrow	*Zonotrichia capensis*	●	●		
White-throated Sparrow	*Zonotrichia albicollis*	●			
Grasshopper Sparrow	*Ammodramus savannarum*		●	●	
Saffron Finch	*Sicalis flaveola*	●	●	●	
Blue-black Grassquit	*Volatinia jacarina*		●	●	
Cardinal Grosbeaks and allies – Cardinalidae					
Summer Tanager	*Piranga rubra*		●	●	
Scarlet Tanager	*Piranga olivacea*	●	●	●	
Western Tanager	*Piranga ludoviciana*			●	
Rose-breasted Grosbeak	*Pheucticus ludovicianus*	●		●	
Black-headed Grosbeak	*Pheucticus melanocephalus*			●	
Blue Grosbeak	*Passerina caerulea*			●	
Indigo Bunting	*Passerina cyanea*	●	●	●	
Dickcissel	*Spiza americana*	●	●		
New World Warblers – Parulidae					
Ovenbird	*Seiurus aurocapilla*	●	●	●	
Golden-winged Warbler	*Vermivora chrysoptera*			●	NT
Blue-winged Warbler	*Vermivora cyanoptera*	●			
Tennessee Warbler	*Leiothlypis peregrina*	●	●	●	
Northern Parula	*Parula americana*	●	●		
Chestnut-sided Warbler	*Dendroica pensylvanica*	●		●	
Yellow Warbler	*Dendroica petechia*	●	●		
Blackpoll Warbler	*Dendroica striata*	●	●		
Bay-breasted Warbler	*Dendroica castanea*	●	●	●	
Blackburnian Warbler	*Dendroica fusca*	●	●	●	
Magnolia Warbler	*Dendroica magnolia*	●	●	●	
Cerulean Warbler	*Dendroica cerulea*			●	VU
Cape May Warbler	*Dendroica tigrina*	●	●	●	
Black-throated Blue Warbler	*Dendroica caerulescens*	●		●	
Yellow-rumped Warbler	*Dendroica coronata*	●	●	●	
Black-throated Green Warbler	*Dendroica virens*	●	●	●	

		Aruba	Curaçao	Bonaire	GTS
Yellow-throated Warbler	*Dendroica dominica*			●	
Prairie Warbler	*Dendroica discolor*	●	●		
Palm Warbler	*Dendroica palmarum*	●	●	●	
American Redstart	*Setophaga ruticilla*	●	●	●	
Black-and-white Warbler	*Mniotilta varia*	●	●	●	
Prothonotary Warbler	*Protonotaria citrea*	●	●	●	
Worm-eating Warbler	*Helmitheros vermivorum*		●	●	
Northern Waterthrush	*Parkesia noveboracensis*	●	●	●	
Louisiana Waterthrush	*Parkesia motacilla*	●	●	●	
Kentucky Warbler	*Oporornis formosus*	●	●	●	
Connecticut Warbler	*Oporornis agilis*	●	●	●	
Mourning Warbler	*Oporornis philadelphia*	●	●		
Common Yellowthroat	*Geothlypis trichas*	●	●	●	
Hooded Warbler	*Wilsonia citrina*	●		●	
Canada Warbler	*Wilsonia canadensis*			●	
New World Blackbirds– Icteridae					
Venezuelan Troupial	*Icterus icterus*	●	●	●	
Orchard Oriole	*Icterus spurius*		●	●	
Baltimore Oriole	*Icterus galbula*	●		●	
Yellow Oriole	*Icterus nigrogularis*	●	●	●	
Oriole Blackbird	*Gymnomystax mexicanus*	●			
Yellow-hooded Blackbird	*Chrysomus icterocephalus*		●	●	
Shiny Cowbird	*Molothrus bonariensis*	●	●	●	
Carib Grackle	*Quiscalus lugubris*	●	●	●	
Great-tailed Grackle	*Quiscalus mexicanus*	●	●		
Greater Antillean Grackle	*Quiscalus niger*	●			
Red-breasted Blackbird	*Sturnella militaris*	●			
Eastern Meadowlark	*Sturnella magna*			●	
Bobolink	*Dolichonyx oryzivorus*	●	●	●	
Weavers – Ploceidae					
Village Weaver	*Ploceus cucullatus*	●	●		
Baya Weaver	*Ploceus philippinus*		●		
Old World Sparrows – Passeridae					
House Sparrow	*Passer domesticus*	●	●	●	

BIBLIOGRAPHY

BirdLife International, 2008. *Important Birds Areas in the Caribbean: key sites for conservation.* BirdLife Conservation Series No. 15. Cambridge.

Bond, J. 1985. *Birds of the West Indies* (5th edition). Houghton Mifflin, Boston.

de Boer, B. 2009. *Nos Paranan, Onze Vogels, Our Birds – Curaçao Bonaire, Aruba.* Stichting Dierenbescherming Curaçao.

Evans, P. G. H. 1990. *Birds of the Eastern Caribbean.* Macmillan Education, London.

Hartert, E. 1893. On the birds of the islands of Aruba, Curaçao and Bonaire. *Ibis* (6) 5: 289-338.

Hayes, F. E. 2002. Geographical variation, hybridization, and taxonomy of New World *Butorides* herons. *North Am. Birds* 56 (1): 4-10.

Hayes, F. E. 2006. Variation and Hybridization in the Green Heron (*Butorides virescens*) and Striated Heron (*B. striata*) in Trinidad and Tobago, with comments and species limits. *J. Carib. Ornithol.* 19(1): 12-20.

Hilty, S. L., 2003. *Birds of Venezuela.* Princeton University Press, Princeton and Christopher Helm, London.

IUCN 2010. IUCN Red List of Threatened Species. Version 2010.4. <http://www.iucnredlist.org>.

Kenefick, M., Restall, R. and Hayes, F. 2011. *Birds of Trinidad & Tobago* (2nd edition). Christopher Helm, London.

Ligon, J. 2007. *Annotated checklist of Birds of Bonaire.* http://www.infobonaire.com/pdf/birds-jan2007_annotatedchecklist.pdf

Meyer de Schauensee, R. 1966. *The Species of Birds of South America and Their Distribution.* Livingston, Narberth.

Meyer de Schauensee, R. & Phelps Jr., W. H. 1978. *A Guide to the Birds of Venezuela.* Princeton University Press, Princeton.

Mlodinow, S. G. 2004. First records of Little Egret, Green-winged Teal, Swallow-tailed Kite, Tennessee Warbler and Red-breasted Blackbird from Aruba. *North Am. Birds* 57: 559-561.

Mlodinow, S. G. 2009. Two new bird species for Aruba, with notes on other significant sightings. *J. Carib. Orn.* 22 (2) 103-107.

Nijman, V., Prins, T. G. and Reuter J. H. 2005. Timing and abundance of migrant raptors on Bonaire, Netherlands Antilles. *J. Raptor Res.* 39 (1): 96-99.

Peterson, R. T. 1980. *A Field Guide to the Birds – East of the Rockies.* Houghton Mifflin, Boston.

Prins, T. G. and Debrot, A. O. 1996. First record of the Canada Warbler for Bonaire, Netherlands Antilles. *Caribbean. J. Sci.* 32 (2): 248-249.

Prins, T.G., de Freitas, J. A. and Roselaar, C. S. 2003. First specimen record of the Barn Owl *Tyto alba* in Bonaire, Netherlands Antilles. *Caribbean J. Sci.* 39 (1): 144-147.

Prins, T. G., Roselaar, C. S. and Nijman, V. 2005. Status and breeding of Caribbean Coot in the Netherlands Antilles. *Waterbirds* 28 (2): 146-149.

Prins, T. G., Reuter, J. H., Debrot, A. O., Wattel, J. & Nijman, V. 2009. Checklist of the birds of Aruba, Curaçao and Bonaire, south Caribbean. *Ardea* 97 (2): 137-268.

Raffaele, H., Wiley, J., Garrido, O., Keith, A. & Raffaele, J. 1998. *A Guide to the Birds of the West Indies.* Princeton University Press, Princeton and Christopher Helm, London.

Remsen Jr., J. V., Cadena, C. D., Jaramillo, A., Nores, M., Pacheco, J. F., Pérez-Emán, J., Robbins, M. B., Stiles, F. G., Stotz, D. F. and Zimmer, K. J. 2011. A classification of the bird species of South America, version 8 August 2011. American Ornithologists' Union. (SACC) http://www.museum.lsu.edu/~Remsen/SACCBaseline.html

Restall, R., Rodner, C. and Lentino, M. 2006. *Birds of Northern South America: An Identification Guide.* Volumes 1 and 2. Christopher Helm, London.

Reuter, J. H. 1999. *"Stern" guide to the birds of Aruba.* Private publication.

Rutten, M. G. 1931. Over de vogels van de Hollandsche Benedenwindsche Eilanden (Antillen). *Ardea* 20 (3): 91-143.

Sibley, D. 2000. *The North American Bird Guide*. Christopher Helm, London.

Stoffers, A. L. 1956. *The Vegetation of the Netherlands Antilles. Studies on the flora of Curaçao and other Caribbean islands.*

van Buurt, G. 2005. *Field Guide to the Amphibians and Reptiles of Aruba, Curaçao and Bonaire*. Edition Chimaira, Frankfurt am main.

von Berlepsch, H. 1892. Die Vögel der Insel Curaçao. *Journal für Ornithologie* 40 (197): 61-109.

Voous, K. H. 1955. De Vogels van de Nederlandse Antillen. *Natuurwetenschappelijk Werkgroep Ned. Antillen*, no. 5.

Voous, K. H. 1957. The birds of Aruba, Curaçao and Bonaire. *Studies on the fauna of Curaçao and other Caribbean islands* 7, no. 29.

Voous, K. H. 1965. Checklist of the birds of Aruba, Curaçao and Bonaire. *Ardea* 53: 205-234.

Voous, K. H. 1983. *Birds of the Netherlands Antilles*. De Walburg Press, Curaçao.

Voous, K. H. 1986. Striated or Green Herons in the South Caribbean Islands? *Ann. Naturhist. Mus. Wien* 88/89 (B): 101-106.

Wells, J. V. and Wells, A. C. 2006. The significance of Bonaire, Netherlands Antilles, as a breeding site for terns and plovers. *J. Carib. Ornithol.* 19 (1): 21-26.

INDEX

Actitis macularia 66
Agelaius icterocephalus 156
Ajaia ajaja 52
Alopochen aegyptiaca 162
Amazona amazonica 98
    autumnalis 98
    barbadensis 98
    ochrocephala 98
Ammodramus savannarum 154
Anas acuta 28
    americana 26
    bahamensis 28
    clypeata 26
    crecca 28
    cyanoptera 26
    discors 28
    platyrhynchos 26
Ani, Greater 102
    Groove-billed 102
Anous minutus 90
    stolidus 90
Anser albifrons 22
Antrostomus carolinensis 108
Ara araruana 162
    macao 162
    severus 100
Aramus guarauna 60
Aratinga acuticaudata 100
    pertinax 98
    wagleri 100
Ardea alba 44
    herodias 42
Arenaria interpes 68
Athene cunicularia 104
Avocet, American 64
Aythya affinis 30
    collaris 30
Bananaquit 146
Bartramia longicauda 68
Bittern, Least 42
    Pinnated 42
Blackbird, Oriole 160
    Red-breasted 158
    Yellow-hooded 156
Bobolink 156
Bobwhite, Crested 22
Booby, Brown 40
    Masked 40

    Red-footed 40
Bombycilla cedrorum 132
Botaurus pinnatus 42
Bubulcus ibis 44
Bucephala albeola 30
Bufflehead 30
Bulweria bulwerii 34
Bunting, Indigo 152
Burhinus bistriatus 60
Butorides striata 42
    virescens 42
Calidris alba 72
    alpina 72
    bairdii 70
    canutus 68
    fuscicollis 70
    himantopus 72
    mauri 70
    melanotos 70
    minutilla 70
    pusilla 70
Caprimulgus cayennensis 108
Caracara cheriway 56
Caracara, Crested 56
    Yellow-headed 56
Cathartes aura 52
Catharus fuscescens 130
    minimus 130
    ustulatus 130
Catoptrophorus semipalmatus 66
Chaetura pelagica 108
Charadrius collaris 62
    melodus 62
    nivosus 62
    semipalmatus 62
    vociferus 60
    wilsonia 62
Chlidonias niger 88
Chloroceryle amazona 112
Chlorostilbon mellisugus 110
Chordeiles acutipennis 106
    gundlachii 106
    minor 106
Chrysolampis mosquitus 110
Chuck-will's-widow 108
Circus cyaneus 54
Coccyzus americanus 102
    lansbergi 102

    minor 102
Cochlearius cochlearius 48
Cockatiel 162
Coereba flaveola 146
Colinus cristatus 22
Columba livia 94
Columbina passerina 96
    talpacoti 96
Contopus cooperi 116
    virens 116
Coot, American 58
    Caribbean 58
Cormorant, Double-crested 32
    Neotropic 32
Cowbird, Shiny 158
Chroicocephalus philadelphia 78
    ridibundus 78
Crotophaga sulcirostris 102
    major 102
Cuckoo, Grey-capped 102
    Mangrove 102
    Yellow-billed 102
Cyanerpes cyaneus 148
Cypseloides niger 108
Dendrocygna autumnalis 24
    bicolor 24
    viduata 24
Dendroica caerulescens 136
    castanea 138
    cerulea 142
    coronata 140
    discolor 138
    dominica 134
    fusca 134
    magnolia 140
    palmarum 142
    pensylvanica 138
    petechia 136
    striata 140
    tigrina 140
    virens 136
Dickcissel 152
Dolichonyx oryzivorus 156
Dove, Common Ground 96
    Eared 94
    Ruddy Ground 96
    White-tipped 96
Dowitcher, Long-billed 72

Short-billed 72
Duck, Black-bellied Whistling 24
    Comb 22
    Fulvous Whistling 24
    Masked 30
    Ring-necked 30
    White-faced Whistling 24
Dunlin 72
Egret, Cattle 44
    Great 44
    Little 44
    Reddish 46
    Snowy 44
Egretta caerulea 46
    garzetta 44
    rufescens 46
    thula 44
    tricolor 46
Elaenia, Caribbean 114
    Lesser 114
    Small-billed 114
Elaenia chiriquensis 114
    martinica 114
    parvirostris 114
Elanoides forficatus 54
Elanus leucurus 54
Emerald, Blue-tailed 110
Eudocimus albus 50
    ruber 50
Falco columbarius 56
    peregrinus 56
    sparverius 56
Falcon, Peregrine 56
Finch, Saffron 154
    Zebra 162
Flamingo, American 36
    Caribbean 36
Florisuga mellivora 110
Flycatcher, Brown-crested 116
    Fork-tailed 120
    Olive-sided 116
    Streaked 120
    Vermilion 116
Forpus passerinus 100
Fregata magnificens 38
    minor 38
Frigatebird, Great 38
    Magnificent 38
Fulica americana 58
    caribaea 58
Gallinago delicata 74

Gallinula galeata 58
Gallinule, Common 58
    Purple 58
Gelochelidon nilotica 86
Geothlypis trichas 144
Geranoaetus albicaudatus 54
Glaucis hirsuta 110
Godwit, Hudsonian 68
Goose, Egyptian 162
    Greater White-fronted 22
    Orinoco 162
Grackle, Carib 158
    Greater Antillean 158
    Great-tailed 158
Gracula religiosa 162
Grassquit, Black-faced 154
    Blue-black 154
Grebe, Least 48
    Pied-billed 48
Grosbeak, Black-headed 152
    Blue 152
    Rose-breasted 152
Gull, Black-headed 78
    Bonaparte's 78
    Franklin's 78
    Great Black-backed 82
    Herring 80
    Laughing 80
    Lesser Black-backed 82
    Ring-billed 80
Gymnomystax mexicanus 160
Haematopus palliatus 64
Harrier, Northern 54
Hawk, White-tailed 54
Heliornis fulica 64
Helmitheros vermivorum 142
Hermit, Rufous-breasted 110
Heron, Black-crowned Night 48
    Boat-billed 48
    Great Blue 42
    Green 42
    Little Blue 46
    Striated 42
    Tricoloured 46
    Whistling 46
    Yellow-crowned Night 48
Himantopus mexicanus 64
Hirundo rustica 128
Honeycreeper, Red-legged 148
Hummingbird, Ruby-topaz 110
Hydroprogne caspia 84

Hylocichla mustelina 130
Ibis, Glossy 50
    Scarlet 50
    White 50
    White-faced 50
Icterus galbula 160
    icterus 160
    nigrogularis 160
    spurius 160
Ixobrychus exilis 42
Jacana jacana 64
Jacana, Wattled 64
Jacobin, White-necked 110
Jaeger, Long-tailed 76
    Parasitic 76
    Pomarine 76
Kestrel, American 56
Killdeer 60
Kingbird, Eastern 118
    Grey 118
    Tropical 118
Kingfisher, Amazon 112
    Belted 112
    Ringed 112
Kite, Swallow-tailed 54
    White-tailed 54
Knot, Red 68
Lapwing, Southern 60
Larus argentatus 80
    delawarensis 80
    fuscus 82
    marinus 82
Leiothlypis peregrina 136
Leptotila verreauxi 96
Leucophaeus atricilla 80
    pipixcan 78
Limnodromus griseus 72
    scolopaceus 72
Limosa haemastica 68
Limpkin 60
Macaw, Blue-and-yellow 162
    Chestnut-fronted 100
    Scarlet 162
Machetornis rixosus 116
Mallard 26
Margarops fuscatus 132
Martin, Brown-chested 124
    Caribbean 124
    Cuban 124
    Purple 124
    Sand 126

Meadowlark, Eastern 156
Megaceryle alcyon 112
    torquata 112
Merlin 56
Milvago chimachima 56
Mimus gilvus 132
Mniotilta varia 142
Mockingbird, Tropical 132
Molothrus bonariensis 158
Mycteria americana 52
Myiarchus tyrannulus 116
Myiodynastes maculatus 120
Myna, Hill 162
Neochen jubata 162
Nighthawk, Antillean 106
    Common 106
    Lesser 106
Nightjar, White-tailed 108
Noddy, Black 90
    Brown 90
Nomonyx dominicus 30
Numenius phaeopus 68
Nycticorax nycticorax 48
Nyctinassa violaceus 48
Nymphicus hollandicus 162
Oceanites oceanicus 34
Oceanodroma leucorhoa 34
Oenanthe oenanthe 130
Oilbird 104
Onychoprion anaethetus 90
    fuscatus 90
Oporornis agilis 146
    formosus 144
    philadelphia 144
Oriole, Baltimore 160
    Orchard 160
    Yellow 160
Osprey 52
Ovenbird 146
Owl, Barn 104
    Burrowing 104
Oystercatcher, American 64
Pandion haliaetus 52
Parakeet, Blue-crowned 100
    Brown-throated 98
    Rose-ringed 100
    Scarlet-fronted 100
Parkesia motacilla 146
    noveboracensis 146
Parrotlet, Green-rumped 100
Parrot, Orange-winged 98

    Red-lored 98
    Yellow-crowned 98
    Yellow-shouldered 98
Parula americana 136
Passer domesticus 150
Passerina caerulea 152
    cyanea 152
Patagioenas corensis 94
    squamosa 94
Pelican, Brown 32
Pelicanus occidentalis 32
Petrel, Black-capped 34
    Bulwer's 34
Petrochelidon fulva 128
    pyrrhonota 128
Pewee, Eastern Wood 116
Phaethon aethereus 36
    lepturus 36
Phaetusa simplex 84
Phalacrocorax auritus 32
    brasilianus 32
Phalarope, Grey 74
    Red 74
    Red-necked 74
    Wilson's 74
Phalaropus fulicarius 74
    lobatus 74
    tricolor 74
Pheucticus ludovicianus 152
    melanocephalus 152
Phoenicopterus ruber 36
Pigeon, Bare-eyed 94
    Rock 94
    Scaly-naped 94
Pintail, Northern 28
    White-cheeked 28
Piranga ludoviciana 148
    olivacea 148
    ruber 148
Plegadis chihi 50
    falcinellus 50
Ploceus cucullatus 150
    philippinus 150
Plover, American Golden 60
    Black-bellied 60
    Collared 62
    Grey 60
    Piping 62
    Semipalmated 62
    Snowy 62
    Wilson's 62

Pluvialis dominica 60
    squatarola 60
Podilymbus podiceps 48
Porphyrio martinicus 58
Porzana carolina 58
Progne cryptoleuca 124
    dominicensis 124
    subis 124
    tapera 124
Protonotaria citrea 138
Psittacula krameri 100
Pterodroma hasitata 34
Puffinus gravis 34
    lherminieri 34
Pyrocephalus rubinus 116
Quiscalus lugubris 158
    mexicanus 158
    niger 158
Recurvirostra americana 64
Redstart, American 142
Riparia riparia 126
Rynchops niger 92
Sanderling 72
Sandpiper, Baird's 70
    Buff-breasted 72
    Least 70
    Pectoral 70
    Semipalmated 70
    Solitary 66
    Spotted 66
    Stilt 72
    Upland 68
    Western 70
    White-rumped 70
Sapsucker, Yellow-bellied 114
Sarkidiornis melanotos 22
Scaup, Lesser 30
Scrub-Flycatcher, Northern 114
Seiurus aurocapilla 146
Setophaga ruticilla 142
Shearwater, Audubon's 34
    Great 34
Shoveler, Northern 26
Sicalis flaveola 154
Skimmer, Black 92
Skua, Arctic 76
    Great 74
    Long-tailed 76
    Pomarine 76
Snipe, Wilson's 74
Sora 58

Sparrow, Grasshopper 154
    House 150
    Rufous-collared 154
    White-throated 154
Sphyrapicus varius 114
Spiza americana 152
Spoonbill, Roseate 52
Starling, Common 156
    European 156
Steatornis caripensis 104
Stelgidopteryx ruficollis 126
Stercorarius longicaudus 76
    parasiticus 76
    pomarinus 76
    skua 74
Sterna dougallii 88
    hirundo 88
Sternula antillarum 88
Stilt, Black-necked 64
Stork, Wood 52
Storm-petrel, Leach's 34
    Wilson's 34
Sturnella magna 156
    militaris 158
Sturnus vulgaris 156
Sublegatus arenarum 114
Sula dactylatra 40
    leucogaster 40
    sula 40
Sungrebe 64
Swallow, Bank 126
    Barn 128
    Cave 128
    Chilean 126
    Cliff 128
    Southern Rough-winged 126
    White-winged 126
Swift, Black 108
    Chimney 108
Syrigma sibilatrix 46
Tachybaptus dominicus 48
Tachycineta albiventer 126
    meyeni 126
Taeniopygia guttata 162
Tanager, Scarlet 148
    Summer 148
    Swallow 150
    Western 148
Teal, Blue-winged 28
    Cinnamon 26

    Green-winged 28
Tern, Black 88
    Bridled 90
    Cabot's 86
    Caspian 84
    Cayenne 86
    Common 88
    Gull-billed 86
    Large-billed 84
    Least 88
    Roseate 88
    Royal 84
    Sooty 90
Tersina viridis 150
Thalasseus acuflavidus 86
    maxima 84
Thick-knee, Double-striped 60
Thrasher, Brown 132
    Pearly-eyed 132
Thrush, Grey-cheeked 130
    Swainson's 130
    Wood 130
Tiaris bicolor 154
Toxostoma rufum 132
Tringa flavipes 66
    melanoleuca 66
    solitaria 66
Tropicbird, Red-billed 36
    White-tailed 36
    Yellow-billed 36
Troupial, Venezuelan 160
Tryngites subruficollis 72
Turnstone, Ruddy 68
Tyrannus dominicensis 118
    melancholicus 118
    savana 120
    tyrannus 118
Tyrant, Cattle 116
Tyto alba 104
Vanellus chilensis 60
Veery 130
Vermivora chrysoptera 134
    cyanoptera 134
Vireo altiloquus 122
    flavifrons 122
    olivaceus 122
    philadelphicus 122
Vireo, Black-whiskered 122
    Philadelphia 122
    Red-eyed 122
    Yellow-throated 122

Volatinia jacarina 154
Vulture, Turkey 52
Warbler, Bay-breasted 138
    Black-and-white 142
    Blackburnian 134
    Blackpoll 140
    Black-throated Blue 136
    Black-throated Green 136
    Blue-winged 134
    Canada 144
    Cape May 140
    Cerulean 142
    Chestnut-sided 138
    Connecticut 146
    Golden-winged 134
    Hooded 144
    Kentucky 144
    Magnolia 140
    Mourning 144
    Northern Parula 136
    Palm 142
    Prairie 138
    Prothonotary 138
    Tennessee 136
    Worm-eating 142
    Yellow 136
    Yellow-rumped 140
    Yellow-throated 134
Waterthrush, Louisiana 146
    Northern 146
Waxwing, Cedar 132
Weaver, Baya 150
    Village 150
Wheatear, Northern 130
Whimbrel 68
Wigeon, American 26
Willet 66
Wilsonia canadensis 144
    citrina 144
Yellowlegs, Greater 66
    Lesser 66
Yellowthroat, Common 144
Zenaida auriculata 94
Zonotrichia albicollis 154
    capensis 154